How to
holiday
alone like a
BOSS

*Advice and inspiration for solo
holidaymakers*

Hannah Ireland

Hannah Ireland

The Book Guild Ltd

First published in Great Britain in 2023 by
The Book Guild Ltd
Unit E2 Airfield Business Park,
Harrison Road, Market Harborough,
Leicestershire. LE16 7UL
Tel: 0116 2792299
www.bookguild.co.uk
Email: info@bookguild.co.uk
Twitter: @bookguild

Typeset in 10pt Minion Pro

Printed on FSC accredited paper
Printed and bound in Great Britain by 4edge Limited

ISBN 978 1915853 004

British Library Cataloguing in Publication Data.
A catalogue record for this book is available from the British Library.

For my friend Audrey
1926 – 2022

'That's brave.'

'Just you? By yourself?'

'Isn't it dangerous?'

'Won't you be lonely?'

'Table for one? Just *one*?'

These are all things I have heard time and time again. And, as with many things people tell me (mortgage advisors, pharmacists, etc.), I choose to ignore them.

You're a single person and you have a week or so off work. You ponder what you could do with that time. You might have a quick think through everyone you know, and discount them as holiday companions for various reasons, with the most obvious being that you can't stand them. You could sit at home watching Wimbledon and eating strawberries (actually, that sounds great). Or you've seen *Shirley Valentine* on TV again and are considering taking the plunge and heading away by yourself, but you're feeling a bit uncertain about the whole thing.

I'm here to tell you that if you want to go on holiday alone, you can. This is not a book about travelling. I'm never going to be one of those glamorous people who create that perfect Insta shot at the Taj Mahal. Think more 'Bridget Jones washing her big knickers in the bathroom sink in

Spain'. This book is about how to have a successful holiday alone and provide inspiration on places I feel make good solo destinations. Completely selflessly, I have holidayed alone for the past 15 years, showing great dedication to supporting the global economy, while doing the groundwork for you. This is not intended as a detailed travel guide either, but to motivate and encourage – if I can do it, so can you. You're welcome.

Holidaying alone is not often discussed. Some people's perception is that it's a little unfortunate you are going alone. However, most will admire your independence. You might not go far, but you will still get a break from the routine of everyday life. You will have unforgettable experiences, and learn to enjoy your own company, if you don't already, and – who knows – you might find other people along the way who also appreciate your company. You may even decide that you *prefer* to go alone, and never look back.

The best part of going it alone is that you are unlikely to spend the week with someone who is sulking because you accidentally booked the return flight during a World Cup final.

Life is short. Get out there and enjoy it.

Getting in the right mindset and ignoring judgement

In our society, doing any kind of activity alone that people traditionally do as a group is, sadly, often frowned upon. It seems to make people uncomfortable if you mention you're holidaying by yourself. They feel a little sorry for you. It takes a lot to ignore that and do your own thing. I have always found it interesting that, if you say you're travelling solo around Cambodia for three months, friends will tell you how jealous they are. There's something about heading to Majorca for a week alone that often gets a totally different reaction.

I have become used to doing a lot of activities alone because I find that individuals, almost always through no fault of their own, can let you down. As you get older and people start having children and getting goldfish ('I just can't leave him in case the other one eats him, you see'), this issue usually becomes more difficult. Finding someone who wants to go to the same place as you, with a similar budget and interests, leaves you with a much smaller group to choose from.

If a holiday feels like too big a step, start small. Perhaps try a weekend away in the UK. I hear London is rather fun. A spa break, or a weekend in Brighton. If that still feels too daunting, you can build up to it. Try an activity such as going to the cinema alone. No one sitting next to you checking their phone while others tut. Oh, and the crunching, always the crunching. If it feels strange at first, book a ticket for the back row and slip in after the lights go down, and out again before they go up. Easy.

The theatre is another excellent option. You'll often find one ticket left in a row, making it a bit cheaper last-minute. I've even been to pantomimes by myself several times. The woman with the four-year-old who kept staring at me said she was quite jealous that I could enjoy Anton Du Beke as Buttons without having to take a small child to the toilet every few minutes.

Doing things alone is a life skill, and you never know when you might need it. You shouldn't have to feel you are missing out just because you can't always find someone to join you.

There are so many single people out there and you are not the only one doing this, even if sometimes it feels like it. You may not have a significant other, you are perhaps a single parent (I bow down to you), or you might be coupled up with someone who has different interests. Like everyone else, we all deserve a break! It was a revelation to me that I could go on holiday by myself and not just endure it, but have a good time.

Try not to feel embarrassed. For one, you are unlikely to ever see any of the people you encounter again. Most will think you're amazing for doing something they probably would never feel brave enough to do. They are actually admiring your confidence. Well, that's what I like to think, anyway. I was once standing at the back of a flight across the Atlantic, stretching my legs and chatting to one of the crew. He couldn't believe I was travelling solo to visit what he referred to as 'really small towns', but which to me were mid-size American cities. He called all his colleagues over to meet me. I felt like a celebrity. Still no upgrade to business class, though.

Not every holiday alone will be easy (see my experiences in Majorca and Menorca). Sometimes you might feel a bit lonely, or even a bit sad. Don't despair, though. If you're having a low day, just look around. I guarantee within ten feet you will see at least one couple arguing or sitting in complete silence, or an entire family looking at their phones. See? You feel better already.

TWO
Choosing a destination

My checklist usually goes like this:

- How far do I want to travel?
- What is there to do there?
- Are the flights at reasonable times?
- What am I going to do in the evenings?
- Do I need sun? (Yes. The answer to this is always yes.)
- How much money will they suck out of me for the pleasure of not being at my desk and out of my one-bedroom flat for a week?
- Will I feel safe there?
- How many steps is a supermarket from my hotel and do they have a good patisserie section?

Think about what you want from your week. And be realistic. Sitting on a sunbed reading a book sounds like bliss when you're staring at the rain through your office window in February, but a whole week of that by yourself might feel quite long. The odd museum or boat trip can really break that time up. Or are you only after culture and the thought of fighting for a sunbed at 7:01am makes you shudder? Is there something you really love doing, like walking or horse riding? If so, I'm quite jealous. If I had actually bothered to cultivate some interests throughout my life, then choosing destinations might be a little easier.

You may have somewhere in mind you've always wanted to visit but, if not, browsing the departure boards of your nearest airport is a great way to find a destination you hadn't thought of before. This is how I ended up in Halifax, Nova Scotia.

Don't feel you need to go somewhere exotic or far away just to impress other people. If you discover one spot you are completely comfortable with, go as many times as you like and be welcomed back each year like an old friend. After a global pandemic, I think we're just glad to be allowed out of our front doors, no matter where we go. Remember that you're not doing this for other people, you're doing it for you.

For me, the evenings can often be the most challenging part of a solo holiday (although trying to put sun cream on your own back is no picnic either). I believe it's one of the key concerns preventing people from going away by themselves. You watch couples and families getting dressed up after their day at the beach and you feel left out. Big restaurants especially can be quite intimidating when you're met with much surprise and concern from the waiting staff that you're by yourself.

It's something to think about, if you don't want to spend each night sitting in your room. Although, equally, there is nothing wrong with that at all. My sister called me while I was away in the Canary Islands and asked, 'What are you doing tonight?' I said I was going to put a wash on and watch Netflix. There was quite a long pause and then: 'So, you're doing what you'd do at home?'

Yes, yes I am.

Cities are a good option because you can spend the evening at a show or wandering round the livelier areas, just soaking up the atmosphere. Choose outdoor restaurants where you can sit and watch the world go by, or small cafes where it seems I'm in good company being by myself.

Even a hotel with a balcony can make you feel part of what's going on and not stuck in your room. Just don't make the mistake I did when in Valencia, of getting a hotel room with no windows for the sole reason that it also offered a roof-top pool. Sometimes simply being around other people is enough, even if you choose not to engage with them. That's why I enjoy a trip to a supermarket so much.

I find that outdoor eateries are a lot easier as, although you have your phone or a book to settle in with, you can just sit and watch the world go by. Play a game of 'What will that person look like when they're old'. Or make some big life decisions, then promptly change your mind as soon as you get home and wonder what on earth you were thinking. It must have been all that sun.

The added cost of a holiday alone

The first thing you are going to have to come to terms with, is that it will be more expensive to go on holiday by yourself.

You will also almost always forget to change the box on the travel website that has kindly already been completed for you with 'Two travellers', leading you to think you got a fantastic deal – until you get to the payment page.

There are some places which cater for single people through the infamous single supplement, but I prefer to have more freedom in my choices. Unfortunately, that means you will probably be paying for a room for two by yourself. However, if you come round to my way of thinking, you can view this as the price of not having to put up with anyone else and their tendency to leave towels on the bathroom floor for the duration of the stay.

I book all my trips on well-known sites, as the hotel or apartment and flights are usually cheaper if booked together. They also do multi-city flights, which can come in handy if you're trying to squeeze more than one destination into your week off.

Always check the accommodation's own website for deals. You can, of course, rent an apartment, but depending on where I am, I quite like the company and safety to be found at a hotel. I do lots of research beforehand: you've saved up for this holiday and have to pay for the bloody room by yourself, so it might as well be somewhere that doesn't have brown stains all over the bedding. If a reviewer has given a hotel one star because the breakfast was cold one day, don't let that put you off if it seems to offer everything else. Luckily, I've never really had a bad hotel experience. Unless you count having no windows.

Plan your trip from the airport to your accommodation. I prefer to arrive during daylight hours if the place is unfamiliar.

There's nothing worse than being the last person in a small airport at night on a public holiday, with no phone reception, wondering how on earth you're going to find some transport.

If a train or bus into town isn't obvious, book a transfer with a reputable company. Safety first, people! If you don't want to hire a car and would like someone else to do the driving, look for day trips where you will be picked up and dropped off from your accommodation. Warning: this will probably mean that you will have to talk to other people, though. And Tammy-Lynn from Ohio might want to stay in touch. *Shudder*.

Staying safe when holidaying alone

It almost goes without saying but things can go wrong, so make sure you have travel insurance. Do read at least the highlights of what your policy entails and don't just buy it because it's cheap and was the first one on the list.

I leave any cards I'm not going to use at home, as you probably won't need your Tesco Clubcard in Texas. Leave a spare key with a friend or at work, in case your bag goes missing while you're away. Never take all your money when you go out, and always put any valuables right at the bottom of your bag. Think about getting one of those cards that you can load currency onto. Stand in a shop doorway to consult Google Maps instead of waving your phone around like a very obvious tourist, who is just waiting to have it grabbed from their hand. Most importantly, I generally try to walk with a sense of purpose plastered all over my face. It seems to work – people are always asking me for directions.

You do have to be a bit more wary when you're by yourself. Don't stray down dark alleys in Barcelona or take early morning walks along deserted roads in America. I have had one or two occasions when I realised I had put myself in a situation that I probably shouldn't have, such as going for an early morning stroll in Florida (jet lag) to look for some illusive fruit at the 7-Eleven. A car slowed down and drove beside me for a short time, until another appeared. Lesson learnt.

Make sure you know how to make an emergency call on your phone. Be vigilant and don't allow yourself to be distracted. Do not fall into a false sense of security just because you're on holiday. However, equally, you should not let fear overtake your trip either. Like anywhere in the world, there are good people and bad but, in general, I've discovered that you will always find someone to help you if you're stuck.

That's the serious part over, I promise.

THREE
Entertaining yourself

The joy of holidaying alone is that you can plan to do as little or as much as you like without taking anyone else's feelings into consideration. There's nothing quite like waking up in the morning and not knowing what the day will bring. However, if you're anything like me, you will put a lot of pressure on yourself to do absolutely everything available in the area within the first 24 hours, and then wonder what you're going to do for the rest of the trip.

I love the feeling of going on an adventure somewhere you don't know anyone. It's a sense of freedom unlike anything else. You can be who you want to be. I've never been brave enough to *actually* pretend I'm someone else though, because you never know when they really will need a doctor on the plane.

Get yourself a guidebook before you go. Pick out what you most want to see and do. If it feels more reassuring, plan out an itinerary. Download all those boxsets you never have time to watch. Take a few books and those trashy magazines you might not buy at home (My now not-so-secret pleasure – the ones that tell fables of people leaving their partner for their mum's sister's ex-boyfriend). Be lazy or be active – who is going to judge you?

There will be activities that you might think you're not confident enough to do by yourself at first. Do consider attempting them, as the worst that can happen is you'll just feel a bit embarrassed. However, if I can play mini golf alone, so can you.

Don't be afraid to talk to other people. Sometimes you won't feel like it. However, even a short exchange can break up the day, and remind you that you know how to formulate sentences. On the plus side, not speaking so much will mean fewer wrinkles, so there's another bonus to holidaying alone. You never know what might happen: you may even end up having a great night out in Malta with a French oncologist, a tourist from Algeria and a horse named Billy. My eulogy is practically writing itself at this point.

FOUR
Destination inspiration for solo holidays

Here are the destinations in the UK, Europe and North America, where I have holidayed alone over the past 15 years. I have never taken more than a week and a half off work for any of these trips, just in case you were wondering. I'm still waiting for sabbaticals to be introduced. I think it might be a long wait.

Some were places I have always wanted to see, and others were booked out of a sense of simply not knowing where else to go. Several have become firm favourites that I never shut up about, and others were nice to experience once, but I won't be heading back any time soon.

The information included might change over the years but was accurate at time of writing. Get a properly researched guidebook before going. I won't even be offended. However, if you are struggling to think about where to start, and feeling a little daunted by the whole thing, I hope the following destinations will provide some inspiration.

A point of warning, if you are heading to this area and you have the kind of hair that Monica in *Friends* experiences in Barbados ('It's the humidity!') then you might want to take something to tie it up with. As well as a hand fan, and something to continuously wipe the sweat off your back.

Nice

I have been to this area three times on my own. I think it's probably my favourite place in the world. However, full disclosure, I did live in France for a few years. Although as far from the South as you can get. Thanks, Mum and Dad.

The first time I went I stayed in Villefranche-sur-Mer,

for the sole reason that it is where *Dirty Rotten Scoundrels* with Steve Martin and Michael Caine was filmed. Yes, that is the incredibly scientific way I choose some of my holiday destinations. The second and third times, I stayed in Nice itself. I guess I had more money by then. I would recommend doing this, if you can, as Villefranche, while lovely, felt a little isolated.

Tende

Nice itself is pleasant to wander around for the day and you can feel part of the action sitting by the beach on the Promenade des Anglais, a people-watchers' paradise. The parasailing is incredibly entertaining, and you might want to bring some popcorn as you find yourself judging the landings in the manner of an Olympic commentator.

However, the best thing about this area is how easy it is to get a train or bus to other places along the coast. You will, however, spend approximately 40% of each day *waiting* for this public transport.

During my first two trips, I covered St Paul de Vence, where the artist Chagall lived for 20 years, and the neighbouring Vence. My interesting titbit about Vence is that Richard and Judy apparently have a home there, so be on the lookout.

I have also been to Menton, Cagnes-sur-Mer to look around Renoir's beautiful house and gardens, Cap Ferrat to marvel at how the other half live, Beaulieu-sur-Mer for the beach, and Eze Village for the view (get the bus up to it from the station – only attempt the walk if you have the right gear and supplies, and it's under 22 degrees). I also took a trip to Monaco, which doesn't live up to the hype, in my opinion, unless you want to walk the Formula 1 track, and spent a few hours in Cannes, which is very lovely, although I had an eye infection that day, so could only see 50% of it.

By my third trip I thought I had seen most of what Nice and the surrounding area had to offer. I was wrong! Quite by chance I came across Nice Castle Hill and gardens. I greatly enjoyed trekking up many, many steps in extreme heat to get to the top, as the lift was closed because of the pandemic. It was *just about* worth it. I also discovered Roquebrune-Cap-Martin, which has a gorgeous little beach down quite a few steep steps from the station. It's the kind of place where effortlessly cool French families spend August. Even when I lived in France, I was never one of those people. Finally, I hopped on a boat trip from Nice harbour, which is a nice way to spend an hour and have Bono's house in Villefranche-sur-Mer and Elton John's splendid abode on a hill pointed out to you.

The absolute best thing I did was *Le Train des Merveilles* – the Train of Marvels. Little known to tourists, the line loops from Nice-Ville station deep into the Italian Alps. There are a few stops along the way, including the beautiful Breil-sur-Roya, with the final being Tende, where you have a few hours for a wander before going back. I mostly remember the great boulangerie by the main square. Be warned that there are only a few trains a day, so don't get caught out. There's not loads to see, but an interesting little museum as well as some stunning views from the town. It's a lovely way to escape the heat of Nice, and there is someone providing commentary on one of the earlier trains. If you love viaducts and tunnels, and who doesn't, then it's the day out for you.

Nice is an easy place to blend in with your surroundings. There are plenty of bars and cafes where being alone is effortless. I never feel quite so sad to leave somewhere as I do Nice. Luckily, it is only about 20 years before I can start scouting for retirement properties. And even less time if this book sells well.

Nova Scotia, Canada

Once upon a time, I was browsing the departures board in Gatwick for holiday inspiration when the destination 'Halifax' jumped out at me. Oooh, I thought, West Yorkshire might be nice at this time of year. Then I realised it was Halifax in Nova

Scotia. Which is in Canada. Which is that big country on top of the USA.

Speaking with other travellers, I realised it's not the most *obvious* holiday destination. 'Where's that, then?' was the general response.

Intrigued, I thought I would go check it out and see what's what, and so I left the hottest bank holiday on record behind me, to catch a direct flight from Gatwick to Halifax. I arrived to 17 degrees and drizzle, thinking this was a massive mistake and what on earth will I do for a week? Here are my findings.

There *is* enough to do there! I spent my holiday doing activities that depended on the weather, which is very changeable. Hurricane Dorian hit a week after I left. I still regularly check the weather there on my phone and it does seem to be snow one day and swimsuit weather the next. A little like London in August.

On the warm days I enjoyed boat trips and spent time reading in the beautiful Public Gardens down on the Waterfront, or visiting the Halifax Citadel National Historic Site. On the cold, grey and tropical cyclone days, I explored the museums and watched TV in my room – it *is* a holiday after all, and how else would I get through the new series of *Peaky Blinders*?

One of my favourite parts of the trip was learning more about the folk artist Maud Lewis at the Art Gallery of Nova Scotia. Her tiny house is actually *in* the museum. The poverty she lived in while producing such joyful works of art is quite astonishing. I wish I had purchased more prints of her paintings, as they have proved harder to find back home. I have one framed in my living room and it gives me a warm glow every time I look at it.

Halifax itself has a very interesting history, including its connection to *Titanic*, and the Halifax Explosion of 1917, when a French cargo ship laden with high explosives collided with a Norwegian vessel. You can find out more about both at the excellent Maritime Museum, which has some artifacts from *Titanic* on exhibit. The Canadian Museum of Immigration at Pier 21 is also worth a visit, as every immigrant to Canada arrived through this location until 1971, and you can hear the experiences of those who made the journey.

Peggy's Cove

Peggy's Cove

There are quite a few boat trips available in the summer season. These include the *Harbour Hopper*, but I tried the coastal nature tour instead, which lasted two and a half hours. Some beautiful scenery, although we didn't see any minke whales or dolphins as they had the day before. I wonder if they tell everyone that. There is a cheap ferry across the water to Dartmouth, which takes less than 15 minutes, but I did see a harbour seal playing in the water, which is more than I saw on the C$50 coastal tour. Dartmouth is quite pleasant for a coffee and a wander around a farmers' market.

If you want to get out of Halifax and see a little more without having to hire a car, there is at least one company, *Alternative Routes*, which will pick you up, take you sightseeing, and bring you back. As part of a small group, you will get to see places like Peggy's Cove, Lunenburg, Mahone Bay and the Annapolis Valley. Peggy's Cove is quite moving as it's where Swissair flight 111 crashed in 1998. I was told that many of the fishermen, who still live and work there, set out immediately to see if they could help. There is a memorial to the victims just along the road.

You can also stop off at one of these places for a night or two and be picked up again when you're ready. *Alternative Routes* is essentially a knowledgeable taxi service shared with other holidaymakers.

If you are keen on the *Titanic* connection, get the bus to Fairview Lawn Cemetery, where over 100 victims are buried. It's a poignant experience, although a slightly sombre way to spend part of your holiday ('I could be at work right now but instead I'm in a graveyard'). You'll spend the bus journey back googling their sad stories.

Most people use Halifax as a stopover on their way to and from other places. I didn't meet anyone else who was just staying there. I obviously like to be different. Other popular choices appeared to be Montréal, Québec City, Newfoundland and Prince Edward Island (known as PEI or *Anne of Green Gables* country).

The main reason Nova Scotia stands out for me is that I've never met such friendly people. From the local bus drivers making sure I got off at the right stop to the hotel staff, everyone was lovely. They made this single person feel very much at home, and that I was probably very interesting and brave for going there by myself. I'm already planning my next trip, in search of my very own Gilbert Blythe.

Florence, Italy

A guidebook on Tuscany was the very first one I ever bought. I had visions of being swept away on a romantic holiday à la *Much Ado About Nothing*, the film with Ken and Em. However, by 2018 the guidebook was outdated, and I was 38 and single. So, I decided to just go anyway.

I went to Florence for an August bank holiday, which anyone who has ever been there told me was the Worst Idea In The World. My strategy was to get up early and do the touristy stuff and be done by lunchtime to avoid the hordes. You can book yourself time slots for tickets to the big museums, or you can stand around in 33 degrees for two hours waiting to get in – your choice.

Florence

Florence is not very big; you can walk across town in less than half an hour, and that's from someone who sets their walking speed at 'amble'. I started with the Uffizi Gallery, to see ~~Ryan Reynolds filming *6 Underground* for Netflix outside~~ priceless works from the Italian Renaissance.

The Duomo is also a must-see and you can queue (for around a week, it seemed) to go inside, or buy a ticket that allows you to skip the queue and also climb nearly 500 steps to the top. How nice of them to let you pay for that. If you want to see Michelangelo's *David*, then head to the Galleria dell'Accademia. It's bigger than you think. I mean the statue, of course.

I discovered that the best thing about Florence is that it is a great base to visit other places. The trains are quite unlike British ones – reliable and cheap. They are also safe to take by yourself. You can easily book online beforehand, although the queue for tickets wasn't long. I started with a trip to Siena which, as a UNESCO World Heritage Site, was glorious, and helped me hit around 25,000 steps that day. I soon learnt that, in general, the buildings of the 13th century were constructed a long way away from train stations. I'm only joking. It wasn't actually that far.

I then went to Pisa to see the Leaning Tower, which is surprisingly small but also astoundingly beautiful. I felt like I had already seen it in books and on TV, but no. It truly is a marvel. The rest of Pisa is also worth a look on the walk from the train station: I got off at Pisa Centrale but there is a station closer to the tower, Pisa San Rossore. From Pisa I went to Lucca, where Puccini was born. Another gorgeous

Siena

walled city, and quite quiet compared to the other two. Worth the very cheap train ticket from Pisa anyway.

I crammed a lot into my five-night stay and still had time to lounge by the pool, eat an indecent amount of pizza, watch incredible sunsets, order gelato in what turned out to be broken Spanish, fend off suggestive comments from Italian men and read a couple of books. I also translated for an English family when their son scraped a lot of skin off his leg and the only person around to help was a French nurse. There are just *so* many interesting ways to meet people.

My hotel had an amazing view of Florence. I ate my breakfast every morning on the terrace, looking out over the city while trying some of my Italian on the poor waiters, who were very sweet and looked after me well. The only better view is from Piazzale Michelangelo, which is a bit of a hike but worth it. I heard there was a bus but what's a holiday without suffering over 100 deep steps in incredible heat, stopping every so often to pretend to check your phone when you're actually just pausing to get your breath back and wishing you weren't quite so unfit.

The only thing I didn't get to do was head out into the countryside, especially the Chianti Hills (or Chiantishire as it is known, for its popularity with the Brits) as that would require a car, and so my romantic ideals of Tuscany did stall a little there. Luckily, I went back with family in 2022 and was able to see a bit more, including the beautiful Montepulciano.

However Villa Vignamaggio, one of the filming locations which features in my *Much Ado* fantasies, was closed for renovations, so I missed out on having the full experience of deceit, heaving bosoms and fanciful language. Don't worry, my beautiful Florence. I'll be back next time Ryan R decides to film there.

Jersey, Channel Islands

I spent eight years living in France, and Jersey was the location of our nearest Marks & Spencer. We would get up at 4am to take the boat from St Malo, spend the whole day shopping, then catch the 5pm boat back to France. It was rather a long way to go for a Battenberg cake.

We also enjoyed a few holidays on Jersey, and when I was in my late teens, I spent a summer working there. However,

Mont Orgeuil

I didn't fully appreciate much more than the local pub and Topshop.

At the grand age of 41, I went back over the August bank holiday in 2021. With all the Covid restrictions still in place, it felt like quite a safe option. The weather was fantastic, and I discovered a Jersey that I hadn't been aware of. The history! The beaches! The odd French-sounding place names that confuse even the French!

My only warning about Jersey is the traffic. I hadn't visited in five years, and it was so much worse. It takes a long time to get anywhere. You often sit on the bus thinking how you'd already be there if you had walked instead.

Here are my Jersey must-sees:

St Aubin. Gorgeous little port and town in St Brelade. Easy bus along the coast from St Helier but also within walking distance. The bus gets stuck in traffic, so it might be faster to get some steps in anyway.

La Corbière Lighthouse. I've seen it before but walked out to it this time (you can't go inside). Even though you know the tide isn't coming in yet, there's a plaque on the wall dedicated to a man who died trying to save someone who drowned in this spot, and it certainly adds a little *frisson* to your walk.

St Brelade Bay. I couldn't believe the beach at this spot. It felt like I had gone somewhere really exotic – people thought I had been to Thailand from the photos. A long stretch of very clean sand, with lots of places to eat and a beautiful old church in the background. Highly recommended.

St Brelade Bay

Mont Orgueil Castle. Over 800 years old with amazing views. Free guided tours. On a clear day you can see Normandy. I waved, but no one waved back.

The War Tunnels and German Underground Hospital. I find it endlessly fascinating that Jersey was occupied during the Second World War. Come and discover the story of life in Jersey during that time. Perhaps not for the claustrophobic.

St Elizabeth Castle. Built on a rocky islet in St Aubin's Bay, Elizabeth Castle has defended Jersey for more than 400 years. You can take the amphibious Castle Ferry or walk out along the causeway at low tide. CHECK THE TIDE TIMES if you don't want to end up on the news.

Havre des Pas bathing pools and beach. Across the road from my hotel; my very own original Victorian bathing pool and lido. What a way to start the day. It made me want to move out of London immediately.

St Helier. Lots of good shopping and restaurants in a nice pedestrianised area. The scene of much of my teenage heartbreak. Topshop long gone. Sad face.

Jersey is a great start to holidaying alone. It's basically like being at home but not. The only issue, and I know this will be a big deal for some people, is that they don't use Sparks cards in their Marks & Spencer.

I know.

Chicago, USA

Chi Town. The Windy City. Chicagoland. City of Broad Shoulders. City of the Big Shoulders. I didn't even make these last two up. *Chicago*.

I was wary of visiting Chicago due to the levels of violence you regularly hear about in the news. However, several of my friends have lived there and persuaded me otherwise. I'm very glad I finally listened. I spent five nights there in the first week of July 2018 and had a brilliant time.

The architecture is amazing. Just incredible. If, unlike me, you are knowledgeable about this type of thing, you will get even more out of it. Make sure you do an architecture sightseeing tour. I did mine with *Seadogs*, who also offer a combined speedboat trip along the lake. It's not that fast, but

Chicago

there is the alternative of a super-scary one that I could only watch from the shore, while still feeling a little queasy just listening to the screams. I still hear them in my nightmares. There are several boat companies to choose from, although I did find them quite expensive, so look online for discounts.

My other favourite activities included a visit to the Art Institute of Chicago, which was a lot bigger than I thought, so plan what you want to see strategically. You might recognise it from *Ferris Bueller's Day Off*. I took a tour of Wrigley Field, the second oldest baseball field in the US. Baseball isn't a sport I'm exactly knowledgeable about, but I still enjoyed hearing the history of it in a *Field of Dreams* kind of way. I also took a stroll through Millennium Park to see the iconic Cloud Gate statue (aka 'The Bean'), and had a few moments of relaxation on one of the city's beaches.

As long as you can cope with heights, head to either the John Hancock Tower or the Willis Tower for some views. The locals made it very clear they feel the Willis Tower should still be called the Sears Tower. This was a very passionately debated subject. I was in no way qualified to comment but I'm very good at nodding and looking sympathetic. I am also pretty good with heights, but the 94th floor of John Hancock still made me feel a little light-headed. I felt better when many grown men struggled to stand near the edge. You can even do the Tilt Ride if you are so inclined (no pun intended), but standing on see-through glass and leaning 30 degrees off the top of a building isn't really my idea of fun. Though you do get a sticker for the achievement, so that makes it absolutely worthwhile.

If shopping is your thing, you have come to the right place. Hit the Magnificent Mile, or Mag Mile in local-speak, to spend the big bucks. Don't be scared to use the subway. It's very easy and economical, and you can buy their version of an Oyster card to make it even more so.

It's refreshing to go somewhere that isn't full of European tourists, like New

Chicago

York. However, I did miss my fellow countrymen and women during the World Cup games, when everyone else was cheering on Colombia.

All in all, I found Chicago to be a great destination as a lone holidaymaker and I will be heading back there in 2023. You'd have no reason to go to the areas which, unfortunately, may not be so safe. Just be as careful as you would anywhere else, but don't let that put you off going, if only for the deep-dish pizza.

Gran Canaria, Spain

May 2022. I booked the first week of the month off in January and now it is three days before that annual leave starts, and I have yet to organise a holiday. Europe is still decidedly chilly, but I'm also feeling lazy and don't want to travel too far. It's a real first-world problem.

Desperate to just go *somewhere*, I settled on Gran Canaria. I stayed in Maspalomas, which felt like a compromise between the too quiet and too noisy areas. Although, actually, Maspalomas is pretty much the noisy area, but I chose a little apartment down a quiet street with my own garden. However, it turned out that Maspalomas that week was also the monkeypox outbreak capital of the world. I sure know how to pick 'em.

I wanted some warmth and Gran Canaria certainly provided that – it was 32 degrees on bank holiday Monday. I was pleasantly surprised, though, that there were also a few things to do, other than visit their excellent mini marts.

I started with the sand dunes of Maspalomas. Who knew? I walked down to take a look, although you're only allowed on dedicated paths these days because of attempts to keep them at peak health. However, that didn't stop most people from wandering all over them. The sand had its revenge as it burnt the soles of their feet, ha ha ha. You can still get wonderful views from the paths. The Atlantic Ocean is apparently responsible for their formation. They didn't just blow over from the Sahara as so many think. Obviously not me. I would never have thought that.

Maspalomas dunes

Puerto de Mogán

I also did a little day trip to Puerto de Mogán, a picturesque fishing village with a small beach and nice shops. It's very popular with tourists, and crying British children in particular.

Gran Canaria is where I finally tried mini golf by myself. I felt a bit weird about it but thought, 'why not'? I really enjoyed no one observing my lack of skills, telling me that I wasn't doing it right and giving me useless pointers. Instead, I joked with the British tourists ahead of me that they were about to see some 'Tiger Woods-level sh*t'. That might have been a slight overstatement: when I got to the end, they gave me another round for free. I'm still not sure how to feel about that.

I ignored the nightlife. I was happy sunbathing, swimming, people-watching and enjoying restaurants where waiters half my age asked how come they'd never seen me around here before and did I want to go for a drink. I was quite pink from the sun and perspiring more than a little, with the addition of 'huge humidity hair' once again, so that was a totally unbelievable request. *Gracias* for the confidence boost though chaps.

The Lake District, UK

With some annual leave to use up, I decided on a UK holiday in October 2017. My first ever. After a lot of research, I picked the Lake District. I'll admit that I wasn't *completely* sure where this was. Only when my train left Euston station did I start to get a good sense of where I was going. Look, I didn't spend all my formative years here and my geographical knowledge

Lake District

of this country is quite sketchy. I do some more nodding and smiling when people tell me where they are from.

I based myself in Keswick, which is a pretty wee town. There are convenient buses which will take you right through the Lake District and back, although they drive far too fast for my liking, and I wasn't the only one wondering if I'd live long enough to actually see a lake. I guess I'm more used to standstill London traffic. I started in Grasmere, which was my favourite spot, although it was also where I was lucky enough to see a middle-aged couple skinny-dipping and, I realised later, catch it on camera.

I met a fully-clothed couple and their dog, and we walked to Ambleside together (nearly four miles; thank goodness I'm well-practised in conversations with strangers), before going

Lake District

on to Windermere and Bowness. I'd like to go back to both spots as I didn't stay long. It was raining and I'd seen enough lakes by the time I got there. It's all very easy and accessible, with lots of people dressed for hiking but actually just visiting garden centres.

I was fairly lucky with the weather as I'm not sure what you would do there if it was pouring the way it was on the day I left. Enjoy your jigsaws, suckers! I bought *Five easy walks around Keswick* from the Information Centre on my first day, to get out and make the most of all that grey-but-dry weather. I guess it depends on what your definition of easy is…I did two of them, plus half of a third, and while I enjoyed them (apart from getting lost after missing a sign when trying to coax a horse into remaining in its field), it was *so* quiet on the routes. They all involved trekking through lonely bits of woodland, and I spent some time googling 'murders in Keswick'.

There didn't appear to have been any so off I went, although I felt a bit anxious at points, which spoilt the enjoyment a little. I guess there are more people out and about in the summer, so that would probably be a better time to go. Anyway, I survived, despite several barbed-wire incidents, and there's nothing like a chip takeaway and a hot shower after walking ten miles.

Another point of interest is a visit to Cockermouth to see William Wordsworth's house and the Derwent pencil museum (yes, really), where you will be given a quiz to complete about graphite. It used to be more valuable than gold, you know. If that's not an educational holiday, I don't know what is.

Philadelphia, USA

By June 2022 I hadn't been to the States in over four years because of that pesky coronavirus. My air miles were looking decidedly dejected.

But never fear! My youngest sister now lives in the US, and I have a lovely American brother-in-law who arranged for me to turn up in their kitchen unannounced, on her 30th birthday. After she'd enjoyed the best possible present (me), and I got over my first ever bout of Covid (absolutely bloody typical), I decided to spend a few days by myself in Philadelphia.

My first thought was 'wow, it's easy to get from the airport into town on a nice train where the conductors open the doors for you'. This is fairly different to the London experience. My second was 'wow, that humidity is something else'. Late June and it was over 32 degrees with 95% humidity every day.

Philadelphia

I had three full days there and packed quite a lot in, especially considering I spent the mornings at the hotel pool, chatting to people from New Jersey and Arizona who were in town to see Mötley Crüe. I've never been asked if I'm Australian with such frequency.

Philadelphia has a fascinating history. Most importantly, it's where you can see the steps from the *Rocky* film. The statue of the man himself had the longest queue of any attraction. If you enjoy watching middle-aged men getting their friends to film them running up steps, then cheering for themselves when they get to the top, this is the place to be. All I could think is that the steps really needed weeding.

The city has more to offer than just steps. My first stop

was Elfreth's Alley. This is often referred to as the oldest continuously inhabited street in America. Gorgeous houses, and it's amazing that people still live in them. From there, I walked down to Penn's Landing and the Delaware River. I paused here to sit in the shade, enjoy the calm waters and the sense of history, before I continued on my way.

Boy, did I walk in Philadelphia. About seven miles a day in the heat and humidity, which was just as well because of the vast amount of pretzel bread I was consuming from Trader Joe's. Oh, and the doughnuts/donuts from the Reading Terminal Market – definitely go there for every type of food you can think of. I tried to avoid heatstroke by getting the hop-on, hop-off bus but they finished around 5pm and I didn't get my ticket until mid-afternoon, so it was a bit of a waste of money, but convenient if you don't have much time to see the city.

Philadelphia

You see a lot more when you walk anyway, such as an amazing mural paying homage to the firefighters of Philadelphia at 323 Arch Street. I passed Benjamin Franklin's grave nearby, which costs $5 to see, or you can look at it through some bars for free, and maybe just stick your arm through them to get a picture. I wanted to go to the Benjamin Franklin Museum, but they seemed to be ushering people out by 4:30pm. Everything closes quite early. That was mainly an issue as I was lying by the pool until lunchtime, so possibly not their fault.

I queued behind hundreds of loud people all wearing the same T-shirt to see the Liberty Bell – no entrance fee but with airport-style security. After setting off the alarm, they immediately asked if I had a pacemaker. 'No, sir, and surely the buckles on my sandals are a more likely culprit?' This went on for some time until they eventually scanned my shoes. Mystery finally solved. There's some information on the history of said bell, and then you finally get to the real thing. It's basically a bell with a big crack in it. The Americans around me were super excited.

Independence Hall is just across the way from the Liberty Bell. This is where the United States Declaration of Independence and the Constitution of the United States were debated and adopted by America's Founding Fathers (I copied this from the internet, if you can't tell). Their tours were all booked up, but I managed to talk my way in as it was raining and lots of people didn't show. I'm going back to London tomorrow and this will be my only chance to go *ever* (this reasoning had also worked well at Universal Studios, so

I thought I would try it again). Thank you, kind US ranger-type man.

I had a quick look at Betsy Ross' house but didn't go inside. I'd never heard of her before this trip, so I could feel myself learning. She is credited with making the first official US flag. My favourite place to potter around was Society Hill and its historic architecture. I spent a while googling how much these homes cost, just in case they were a bit cheaper than central London (nope). I walked past the home of former president James Madison and his 'famous hostess' wife, Dolley. That's literally how she is described on the plaque. I think I'd want my plaque to say something a little more profound.

There are so many random things I caught on my walks, such as the filming locations from *Trading Places*. I paid a trip to the Curtis Publishing Company on a Sunday and sat by the reception, gazing at the amazing Tiffany glass mural, and then strolled around the empty building feeling like I was in *Mad Men*. I also ended up at a Harry Potter exhibition in the Franklin Institute, where the staff quickly realised I was British. I should have told them I was an extra in the films. I asked them to please not tell anyone I had come all this way to do something I could have done at home. Look, it was raining, OK?

I enjoyed my Philadelphia trip, totally doable by yourself and lots to keep you entertained. Just get up early.

Malta

Malta is my lazy early or late summer sun venue. It's not a long flight, it's pretty much always hot and, best of all, almost all the hotels on the island are only a short taxi ride from the airport. Hoorah!

One thing you'll notice is that there's not much greenery. However, it is still a truly beautiful place, and is home to some of the oldest free-standing structures in the world. The whole island is geared towards tourism. You won't feel like an imposition and people can't do enough for you.

There are tour buses that take you around both sides of the island separately, and plenty of day trips, including being taken to swim in the Blue Lagoon. Or have you ever fancied careering round the island of Gozo in a jeep? Being the only lone traveller, you will have to sit in the front with your eyes shut as it plunges down yet another hill.

The trips are also a great way to meet people, if you want to. I got talking to two women from France and Algeria, who were each travelling on their own. One had sea sickness, which is always a good conversation starter (if you're like

Malta

me, you'll be sick as soon as you step on a boat no matter how many tablets you've taken), and we ended up having a fun night out in Mdina, formerly the island's capital from antiquity until the medieval period, which is particularly lovely at night. One of those ladies still stays in touch all these years later. I must have made quite the impression.

You can sit and read a book in the Upper Barrakka Gardens, mooch about the capital city, Valletta, and its waterfront, or learn about the Great Siege of Malta and the Knights of St John. My favourite spot was Marsaxlokk, a quaint little fishing village with beautifully decorated fishing boats.

Malta also attracts a lot of *Game of Thrones* fans: there are ten different filming locations to see. It's such a shame that the Azure Window on Gozo is no longer standing, after collapsing into the sea in 2017, as it was stunning. Well, *I* saw it while it was still there, and that's all that really matters.

Arizona, USA

Following a brief trip to Seattle, I flew to Tucson (you'd be surprised at how few people can pronounce that correctly: *Too-son*) to be met at the airport by a cowboy who told me I had a nice smile. That's my kind of town.

The idea of going to a ranch came to me when I researched a holiday that wouldn't involve spending *too* much time with other people, but where you wouldn't be lonely either. I was a bit nervous about the horse part of the holiday. I know you're now wondering why I would even consider a ranch. Up until then, I had only had one slightly scary experience on a horse as a teenager. I spent ages trawling Tripadvisor until I found one I liked the sound of, where there were activities other than riding, in case I was still traumatised and that side of things didn't work out. I was also seeking one that had a pool, because that's what all true cowboys and cowgirls need in their lives. With all this in mind, I settled on a ranch near Tucson.

Arizona

I spent just over a week there. In my first few days, the other guests were very into horses, and I felt a bit out of my depth. Some of them ran their own riding schools in the UK and were surprised that I didn't want to spend the whole day on a horse. Towards the end of my time there were more people who, like me, wanted to relax in beautiful surroundings and eat/sleep/swim, and just play at being cowboys occasionally. On the day I had to leave they went on a day trip to the town of Tombstone, and I was really gutted to miss that. Yes, it's a real place.

I took a riding lesson while I was there, but I was still slightly petrified, although I'm not sure why – mine was the only horse that wouldn't move. I did the slow rides instead of the 'horse sliding precariously down rocky hills' ones.

The landscape is another fascinating aspect of Arizona. In June it was hot and very dusty. To get a better idea of my surroundings, I was the only person to decide to join a hike up 'Panther Peak' in 44 degrees, which was worth it for the views – until we ran out of water on the way back. Thank goodness I am a hardy soul, but the guide and I stopped talking to each other about a mile before we got to the car, all joviality gone and just hoping we would survive. Spoiler: we did.

Arizona

There was also regular evening entertainment, which I usually avoid like the plague when I'm on holiday, but there I embraced it all and sat around a campfire singing *Rawhide* with everyone else. It wasn't as fun as it sounds: the smoke from the fire blew in our eyes causing extreme watering and mascara malfunction. My favourite activity was line dancing, as I have no shame in absolutely loving that even when I'm not on a ranch. I did, however, draw the line at handling snakes and spiders part way through the week.

Arizona is where I discovered roadrunners are real, and not just in cartoons, as a baby scooted past me as I sat out on my terrace one evening. However, they don't say 'beep beep'. I met lots of people from all over the globe at mealtimes, although unexpectedly they were mainly Brits, as we are literally *everywhere*. The sunsets were out of this world and the memories of lying outside at night, staring in wonder at the thousands of stars I never get to see in the city, will stay with me forever.

If you're the kind of person who actually knows how to stay on a horse, I couldn't recommend this holiday more. Grab your leather chaps and go. If you're not that into horses, give it a whirl but don't feel bad for sitting by the pool instead.

Devon, UK

During the coronavirus pandemic, I desperately needed to take a break from queuing for toilet roll and to get out of my small flat, where I was beginning to talk to the walls. So, when they finally let us out of lockdown, I decided on my second ever UK holiday in Devon.

I caught a train from central London to Axminster. It chugged through the countryside, and I even saw some ducks next to the tracks. We're not in Victoria station anymore, Toto. When I arrived, I thought I could jump on a bus to my final destination, Seaton. Um, no. No buses on Sundays.

I spent a while calling all the taxi numbers displayed on the wall. Well, both of them. And then desperately looked online for others, when I got their answering services telling me they were closed on Sundays. I had visions of spending the night sleeping on the station floor. Eventually, someone answered and merely an hour and several chasing phone calls later, they turned up.

After arriving in Seaton, I stayed opposite the seafront and enjoyed amazing weather, which was unusual for the summer of 2021. When I was a kid, we spent our holidays looking for fossils on the beaches in that area, so I decided to do that again 35 years later. I still didn't find any.

I got the bus to Lyme Regis in Dorset, scene of my fossil failure all those years ago. Lovely for a sit on the sand, lunch in town, and a tour of some of the scenes from Jane Austen's *Persuasion*. Ah, Captain Wentworth. I went back to the shop where we used to buy fossils when we didn't find any. Pleasing to see it is still there, and that parents are still buying fossils to bury, and con their kids into thinking they've found some.

To get my steps in and compensate for all the ice cream, I walked from Seaton to Beer. You definitely need to do this, although the hilly section is not for the faint-hearted in sunny weather. On the way back you smile knowingly at the people coming up, and mutter a wry 'Don't worry, you're nearly there!'. The views are wonderful, especially of the beach at Beer.

Beer Beach

Adding to the excitement, I went to *Pecorama*. One of my brothers-in-law told me he used to go there all the time as a kid. Lovely gardens and views, but the ultimate attraction is the Beer Heights Light Railway. I was not at all embarrassed to be the only adult without a child riding on a little train. It was great fun and I have since been considering whether I could get a model railway into my loft. The exit takes you through a shop for train enthusiasts. I really needed someone to take my credit card off me at that point.

In the same vein, I took the Seaton tram to Colyton. This is the big attraction in Seaton. They are almost childlike in size: at 5ft 7", I had to almost bend in half to get down the stairs. There are pretty views and abundant birdlife to see on the short journey. Colyton is really nice for a wander and a look in the estate agents' windows, to daydream about owning a little cottage there, where you'll be driven mad by tourists like me staring through your windows.

I would definitely go back and see more of Devon. Everyone is so friendly. When I returned to London, I found myself smiling more at people as they walked past, and occasionally saying hello. That lasted a whole two days because no one answered back, and they looked like they may report me to the police.

Seaton Beach

Rome, Italy

Rome had been on my list for a long time. I knew I would have to brace myself for a lot of walking and sightseeing in hot weather, so I decided the best possible time to go was as soon as we were allowed on a plane during the global pandemic, and I was right! It was pretty much deserted. I did feel terrible for the businesses of Rome, suffering from the lack of tourists. They actually seemed genuinely pleased to see me.

Apart from having my temperature taken every time I set foot on a train or in a museum, it was all pretty 'ordinary' for the most unusual time in our lives. I watched people run for the train, then come to a sliding halt to have a handheld thermometer pointed at their heads. I stayed for a while just to see if anyone failed (they didn't).

Rome

What a place. I packed loads in and walked and walked. My highlights and recommendations are:

The Colosseum. Well obviously. I would suggest that you pre-book, but I just wandered over one morning and queued for about 40 minutes, which is apparently unheard of in 'normal' times. This passed pretty quickly, chatting to fellow tourists and fending off annoying people trying to sell 'private tours' (you know, those fun ones where you end up in the back of a van). The inside is as fascinating at you would imagine, and you'll burn off all that pasta on the many steep steps. I can't really describe the grandeur and sense of history. You'll have to go and feel it for yourself.

The Roman Forum. I started up on Palatine Hill, which I would advise if you're after that perfect shot of the Forum. Then it's just many more steps down to the former centre of day-to-day life in Rome. It's like being on the set of the TV show *Plebs*. Totally amazing and a good few spots to just sit and soak up the atmosphere.

Castel Sant'Angelo. This didn't feel as popular in terms of tourists (one rather than three) as it's slightly off the main track. You'll recognise its cylindrical shape, especially if you've watched the film *Red Notice* with Ryan Reynolds and The Rock, and let's face it, who hasn't? Castel Sant'Angelo was commissioned by the Roman Emperor Hadrian as a mausoleum for himself and his family. I subsequently started designing my own. Just a few light sketches for now.

Anyway, you walk down the long, winding dark path where they carried his body. If you're alone like me, you may feel like you're about to be murdered. Don't worry, that's pretty unlikely. Wonderful views of the Vatican too.

Piazza Navona. Great spot for gelato or coffee. Or both.

I tried to go to the Galleria Borghese, which houses a substantial part of the Borghese Collection of paintings, sculptures and antiquities, but the next admission was in five days' time and I would already be back in my flat by then. So, I had a wander and sit-down in the Parco dei Daini instead. So yeah, the lesson here is to think about booking the Galleria ahead of time.

Altar of the Fatherland. I walked round a corner and boom; there it was. Don't laugh please. However, I hadn't read my guidebook yet and, at first, I thought it might be the Pantheon. I said, *don't* laugh. It's also known as the Victor Emmanuel II National Monument and is the best place to enjoy the panoramic scenery of Rome. I remember lots of steps, but also the views of the Colosseum and Forum. You can pay extra to take a glass lift right to the top. I found this slightly terrifying and not at all like *Charlie and the Chocolate Factory*. I had to keep my eyes shut on the way down. I'm not sure it was worth the money, but when in Rome…

The Trevi Fountain. It's in a smaller area than I imagined, with shops just metres away. But absolutely magnificent in an almost unexpected way. I did get slightly irritated by all the ridiculous posing in front of it, but just bought myself an ice cream and adopted a bemused expression to deal with it.

The Trevi Fountain

The Pantheon. This was the *actual* Pantheon and not the fake one I stumbled across on day one. As I went during the pandemic, there were only about three other people inside. The sun caught beautifully through the door as I went in, and it was quite a memorable moment.

Vatican Museums. If you want to see lots of amazing art, gold and of course the Sistine Chapel, then this is the place for you. A really fun pastime is watching people try to take photos in the chapel and then being told off. I saw people attempt to distract the guards while their friend took a picture as well as a mother who was pretending not to, but definitely was…it was all very entertaining. I went during a thunderstorm; make sure you book before you go, unless you want to stand in the pouring rain or boiling sunshine for hours.

I loved my few days in Rome. Obviously, this could have been because I hadn't left my home for over a year. Even so, I smile whenever I think of that trip, as it was exactly what I needed: lots of sun, friendly people, so much to see and do, and loads of carbs. I will certainly make Rome my destination of choice during the next pandemic.

Berlin, Germany

As soon as I arrived in Berlin, I wondered why I'd waited so long to visit. I decided on a trip during a very cold spell in November and had four wonderful days getting to know this fantastic city. You could also think about going a little later to see the Christmas lights, which I hear are magnificent.

Berlin is a very easy place to navigate, especially on the subway. I also spent a lot of time just pottering through the streets, not wanting to miss anything. It was, of course, packed with tourists, so I didn't get to meet many locals.

I started at the Brandenburg Gate. There was hardly anyone else there on that supremely cold evening, as most people had the good sense to be inside, and I got some fantastic photos. Over the course of the next four beautifully sunny days, I headed to see the old crossing point between East Berlin and West Berlin, Checkpoint Charlie, as well as some of the remaining parts of the Berlin Wall. Make sure you visit the Memorial of the Berlin Wall, where I was gripped by stories of how people lived, and sadly died, during that time.

Berlin

A lot of the museums in Berlin are, of course, heart-breaking, and you must brace yourself for what you are about to see and hear. I wasn't sure what to expect when visiting a museum called 'Topography of Terror'. Be prepared to be very moved at this permanent exhibition, which is on the former site of the Gestapo and SS headquarters. You learn about these institutions and the horrific crimes that were planned there. Afterwards, you'll feel compelled to visit, and spend some time in quiet contemplation, at the often-photographed Memorial to the Murdered Jews of Europe.

The DDR Museum is another must-see for an immersive experience of everyday life in the former East Germany. I also spent time at the Reichstag, the neo-Baroque Parliament building, and Museum Island. One island, five museums! You can't say fairer than that. I loved the Pergamon Museum: I always enjoy a good sit-down among classical antiquities to rest my weary feet.

There are also lots of parks, cafes and many nightclubs if you're able to stay awake after 11pm. Berlin is definitely on the short-list for anyone's first holiday alone. My only minor gripe was my inability to ever find a supermarket.

Miami, USA

I'm not ashamed (well, maybe a little) to admit that, when I was growing up, *The Golden Girls* was one of my favourite TV shows. It still is. So, I thought I would head to Miami, which I assumed would be full of plain-speaking, sassy pensioners. I went in early May, and it was scorching. The kind of heat you finally get used to the day before you leave. However, after a long, grey British winter, who's complaining.

I based myself in South Beach, where people-watching is a national sport. I have heard that a woman becomes invisible at 45. In Miami, I would say it is closer to 25. Happily, I am fine with that, although at that time I thought I still had five years to go. There was a lot of flesh on display, and I saw more boobs in that one week than I will probably see for the rest of my life.

Other than the generous availability of partial nudity, I would recommend the useful hop-on, hop-off bus tour. The

Miami

main sights are Wynwood and Little Havana. I didn't find that much to see there: a few gift shops, restaurants and many elderly people playing dominoes and mah-jong. A man got onto our bus to sell us hot chestnuts, which is exactly what I was in the mood for on a scorching day. The bus also takes you to South Beach, Miami Beach and the Art Deco district, which is the best bit of Miami by far (and Instagram heaven). There is a good walking tour if you are confident about being in the sun for long periods of time.

Eating out alone in Miami was incredibly easy. My favourite spot was the News Café, which is famous for being where Gianni Versace had his morning coffee every day. His house, now a hotel, is just along the road from there.

Of course, you have to go to the beach. I have never seen such long stretches of pristine sand. But then I don't get out that much. Even the trash cans had intricate sand designs at their bases. The famous lifeguard huts were re-imagined after Hurricane Andrew in 1992, and are absolutely amazing. I walked for ages, almost passing out in the heat just for a glimpse of the next one. Just. One. More.

The bars and nightclubs don't get going until late in Miami. I didn't really partake, although I did get invited to a pool party. I was sadly a little too sunburnt to attend. I *am* British after all. There are other things to do that I just couldn't find the energy for, such as a day trip to the Bahamas, which according to other tourists can involve 90 minutes of vomiting during the crossing. Fun.

Miami

The weather in May is changeable, so you might be better heading there earlier in the year. It was intense sun and heat one minute, and what felt like the second coming of Hurricane Andrew the next. People were staring enviously (at least I *think* it was envy) at my sturdy British umbrella which I, of course, never leave home without.

All in all, if you can stand the nine-hour flight, and it's not hurricane season, it's a nice alternative to Tenerife.

Barcelona, Spain

Barcelona is one of those places that people assume I have already been to, a bit like Amsterdam (so far, I have only managed their airport. Lots of tulips and clogs). I did actually book a flight there once before, but couldn't face a trip alone with the broken heart I was suffering from at the time. A mere 12 years later, I had recovered and was ready to give it another go.

I flew there in mid-September, with my fingers crossed for sunshine. An easy flight, a bus from the airport, a long walk after getting off at the wrong stop, and I was there. My enthusiasm was slightly muted on arrival at my hotel. I had barely put my case on the floor and searched in my handbag for my passport, before the staff were warning me about the danger of pickpockets. I had of course heard the rumours about that, but their solemnity did catch me a bit off guard. I stepped out of the hotel clutching my valuables to my chest. I think I may have even stuffed my credit card in my bra. Good luck getting to that.

The city is bigger than I anticipated. Even a stroll along the tree-lined Las Ramblas pedestrian street felt quite lengthy, and I found the best way to see it was to reacquaint myself with my old friend, the hop-on, hop-off bus. I swear that company would fold if it wasn't for me.

There are two different routes, and I started using it like a taxi service when I wanted to go to the beach. However, each route is *long*. Especially in evening traffic, so don't do it if you have a plane to catch any time soon. If you have nothing better to do than sit on the top deck enjoying the sun and views, then go for it. I got off at the following stops:

The Sagrada Familia. Gaudi's modernist church has to be seen, though the renovations weren't finished when I was there, so I took some pictures from across the road, trying to find an angle that hid the huge cranes in the background. Book before you go if you want to see inside.

Park Güell. Not that easy to find from the bus stop but just follow other confused-looking tourists and head up the hill. Brilliant views of the city. Book in advance if you want to visit the main park and house. I didn't, so had to content myself with pressing my nose up against the gate, looking at all those laughing, happy tourists who possess foresight.

Casa Batlló. A building that must be seen to be believed. It costs about the same as my first car to go inside. I guess that's fair enough when you're a UNESCO World Heritage Site designed by Gaudi.

La Barceloneta beach. My favourite spot for people-watching and some beach time, although it was slightly ruined by individuals trying to sell me something every 30 seconds.

Tibidabo hill. I was so excited to see this *Friends* reference ('I was hiking through the foothills of mount Tibidabo…') and walked up part of the hill with some French tourists, but none of us could figure out how to get to the theme park and the view. Apparently, you need to use the *Tramvia Blau* (the blue tram), which is a different system to the main transport network. One of those moments when my guidebook and phone both proved completely useless.

The Gothic Quarter (Barri Gòtic). This is where to go to see the Cathedral of Barcelona. Make sure you cover your shoulders and legs, or you will be asked to tie scarves around your body. You'll also see ruins of the old medieval walls, giant medieval churches, a beautiful square called Plaça Reial, and lots of crooked streets. I stopped off at the Barcelona City History Museum too, which was fantastic. Top tip: many Barcelona museums are free on the first Sunday of the month and/or on Sunday afternoons. Of course, I realised this on Monday.

There are loads of other things to do, but I wanted to make sure I had enough time to make full use of the hotel's outdoor facilities. There is, of course, great nightlife in Barcelona, though it is a little hard to feel relaxed enough to head out into the night through the throngs of pickpockets (only kidding, I had no problems – just be vigilant). Or just spend your evenings at the hotel pool bar, which also works well.

The Sagrada Familia

Casa Batlló

Vienna, Austria

I spent Easter in Vienna one year. It was still pretty chilly, and the streets were quite empty. I'm sure it's amazing in the summer. However, I'm not one to let something like the lack of other human beings get me down, so I persevered.

Wandering around the town you will find some incredibly beautiful spots, including the State Opera House, the Rathaus (City Hall), St Stephen's Cathedral and shopping in Stephansplatz. If you are feeling a little more adventurous, get the train out to the Schönbrunn Orangery, which is apparently one of the biggest Baroque orangeries, after Versailles.

I also made a beeline for the Spanish Riding School and their beautiful Lipizzaner horses, which was a real

Vienna

highlight. Make sure you get a ticket in advance, or be prepared to endure the queues. I met a really kind English couple, and we enjoyed a hot chocolate in one of Vienna's famous coffeehouses. It was nice to sit and chat and then say goodbye, without promising to stay in touch. These are my favourite type of people to meet on holiday. They even paid for the hot chocolate.

I went to hear some classical music one night (when in Rome and all that) at the Kursalon Wien. I arrived just as it was about to start and was asked where my guest was several times, as the only empty seat was next to mine. It seems going to listen to music alone in Vienna is just not on. This concert felt like it was very much put on for tourists and I would recommend doing some research to find one that feels a little more authentic.

As far as Vienna being a good solo destination, I would probably go during the summer, when there's more going on. It might be useful to think about brushing up on some basic German too, as English wasn't as widely spoken as in other European cities. One to avoid if you're not keen on the smell of horse manure.

Valencia, Spain

Valencia is a good city for a short break, some sun and a bit of a stroll around an old town. It was one of my first holidays alone and quite an easy place to go to get a tan. However, I had just been through a break-up, and spent quite a lot of time practising silent crying behind my sunglasses.

If you are there in the summer, although they are harder to come by, try to get a hotel with a pool. You are going to need it. The old town is just gorgeous; make sure you stop in

Valencia

at Valencia Cathedral, which is one of the most incredible I have ever seen (and I've seen a lot of cathedrals). The Central Market is also an architecturally beautiful building, where you can buy local produce, including empanadas and fresh fruit. The shopping is great, and I spent half my trip just looking at hats. When I wasn't crying, of course.

Valencia also has some nice beaches, although you are at the mercy of public transport. However, this was before I lived in London, and I was not the confident girl-about-town (ahem) that I am now. In saying that, I only learnt to use buses in London after about six years of being afraid of them. Anyway, I made it to El Cabanyal Beach, and it does what it says on the tin: there was sand and water and that was about it. I'm sure it is more built-up these days. It's a good place to escape the town for a bit.

All in all, Valencia is a good spot for a city break for a few days, and probably best enjoyed in May, June or September. The locals are also very good at pretending they can't see tears streaming down your face, for which I will be eternally thankful.

San Antonio and Austin, USA

I once flew over Texas. It took about four hours. That's just *one* state. Mind. Blown.

On the flight over, the crew were bemused by my tour of what they referred to as 'small towns'. Personally, I wouldn't describe San Antonio or Austin as such (they've obviously never been to rural France). I wasn't sure what to expect of my time in either, but I am on a mission to set foot in as many US states as possible during my lifetime, so it had to be done.

I started off in San Antonio, where I began by ordering some Tex-Mex (*all* my favourite foods are in this dish), had a potter around and then took a boat ride along their famous River Walk. A quick stop at the San Antonio Botanical Gardens before a nosey around the Alamo, which is right in the centre and surrounded by heavy traffic. I sat in its peaceful gardens for some time, enjoying the shade and listening to a talk on its history, before leaving with yet another souvenir mug for the collection in my loft.

I then flew to Austin. You could drive, but I didn't feel confident doing it by myself. Having spent eight hours on a Greyhound bus as a teenager, I wasn't keen to repeat that experience either, and so flight it was.

On my first day I walked to Barton Springs Pool, losing half a stone in sweat in the process. This is an outdoor swimming pool filled entirely with water from nearby natural springs. The tricky thing was trying to watch my stuff while enjoying the water. Like a lot of places in the US, I found it difficult to locate any public transport in Austin, but I did manage to find a bus on the way back. I told the receptionists at my hotel that I had done the 30-minute walk to the pool. From their reaction, you would have thought that I had just completed an ultramarathon on my way to the shops. They probably still talk about it now.

I also decided to go paddling along the Colorado River in a kayak. It was a lovely, peaceful experience. However, I hadn't anticipated how difficult it is to get out of a kayak by oneself. Thanks once again to those passing Irish tourists who managed to haul me out. I was wearing my London

2012 T-shirt in an effort to look like I enjoyed sport (nope).

A uniquely Austin experience is to see the 1.5 million bats which emerge each evening from the Congress Avenue Bridge. They come out at sunset and it's the most incredible sight, unless you're terrified of bats. However, they don't come anywhere near you. There's also a big live music scene if you fancy it, although some of the bars felt a bit intimidating to me. I went to a comedy show instead, but a lot of it went over my head, as it was focused on local politics. I think I'll stick to the bats.

Austin

I had been encouraged to experience a rodeo while in Texas and so I hired a car to reach one in the countryside, not really knowing what to expect. I asked for their smallest vehicle, and it was still bigger than anything I had ever driven. Living in London, I hadn't even put my hands on a steering wheel for over five years. I enjoyed a white-knuckle drive down an eight-lane freeway, got lost, stopped at a show home to get directions, got lost again and pulled in at a small-town gas station, was stared at by the locals and then eventually found the rodeo.

Even the smallest children were dressed like cowboys and cowgirls, and everyone was there to meet up with friends and family. It was interesting to observe what an average Saturday night in that part of the world looks like, making me feel like Louis Theroux. The food part of the evening was great. Then came the entertainment, which began with small children riding sheep as the warm-up act. Poor sheep. Although no child managed to cling on for more than about three seconds. This was followed by horses doing fancy things, before bigger people tried to stay on larger animals. However, I decided I had seen enough, and it was time to attempt the drive back through San Antonio's one-way system before it got dark. Still, at least I didn't hit the deer that ran out in front of my car, and was able to return it, and me, in one piece. I have never felt so relieved to pull into a hotel parking lot.

Texas is a pretty crazy place and won't be everyone's cup of tea. However, I found the people very friendly, and the individuals who run their show homes incredibly helpful if you're lost.

The Amalfi Coast, Italy

Have you ever seen the (pretty awful) film *Only You*? That's right, the movie where Marisa Tomei flits around Italy looking for a man named Damon Bradley. The one thing it has going for it is the scenery, filmed partly as it is on the Amalfi Coast.

I decided to head there, when it couldn't have been hotter, in mid-July. I was looking for some pool time but also a trip to Pompeii, somewhere that has always fascinated me. From my base just outside Sorrento, I was able to hop on a train to get everywhere I wanted to go. The ticket office seemed to be permanently closed and there was no one selling tickets onboard either, so I enjoyed several free rides on graffiti-covered trains.

Amalfi Coast

You will remember from history class that Pompeii was buried under metres of ash after the eruption of Mount Vesuvius in AD 79. It's pretty ghoulish, but you can go and gawp at the excavated ruins of streets and houses. Mount Vesuvius dominates the background, and I kept glancing nervously in that direction. Pompeii was easily the highlight of the trip, but I would recommend going when it's a little cooler as there isn't any shade. There were plenty of stray dogs running around though.

Other than the typical holiday 'tragic scene of many deaths' experience, you can potter around Sorrento and enjoy lunch in the main square. You will probably find that the Italian waiters are very attentive to singletons.

The next spot I made a beeline for was Positano, a cliffside village with lots of steep, narrow streets. The bus from Sorrento was pretty hairy, and I closed my eyes for a lot of it. I met two A&E nurses from Wales and we had lunch together at one of the beach cafes. It took a really long time for a return bus to turn up, which led to much camaraderie as we started planning how we might have to sleep on the beach that night. Big cheers when it finally arrived, with the driver nonchalantly smoking a cigarette and shrugging.

I first read about Capri as a teenager, in Spike Milligan's memoirs. It is where he took Toni the Italian ballerina on holiday and it always sounded magical. While it probably was then, I was a bit disappointed. I should have guessed, but it was *full* of tourists, extremely hot, and apart from an uncomfortable hour on the beach, a bus ride to Anacapri and its beautiful white houses and gorgeous flowers, I found the whole experience really dissatisfying. If you decide to visit, try out of season.

As with anywhere I have been in Italy, the Amalfi Coast makes for a great lone holiday. If nothing else, you might make some new Welsh friends who would be excellent in an emergency.

Dubrovnik

Croatia was a new country for me and one which I was really excited to visit. It didn't disappoint. My taxi driver from the airport was lovely, and that really set the tone for the holiday. The people were incredibly friendly and delightful. Nova Scotia has some competition.

I arrived in early July and the humidity was so high that I gave up trying to look decent by day two. Thank goodness for sunglasses.

This was mainly a pool holiday, but I did leave my sunbed to head to Dubrovnik Old Town. It's beautiful to just walk around, but do also think about exploring the city walls. Perhaps don't attempt it during the midday sun if you want to live to tell the tale, although there are ice cream and drink stops on the way round, thank goodness. Yes, I did it at midday exactly. Try and avoid the Old Town during the peak cruise ship times (10am until 4pm, which is, of course, most of the day) as it's absolutely packed. To get out of the heat and crowds, I popped into the War Photo Limited Museum, where you can see photography exhibits of armed conflicts around the world, including Croatia.

As you'll know by now, I am a sucker for a boat ride and there are lots of companies trying very hard to get your custom in Dubrovnik. I gave in and took one to the town of Cavtat. I ambled around, looking at the super yachts. It's incredibly pretty and the water is pristine. There are lots of other trips to choose from, and you can even head to Montenegro for the day if you so wish. I noticed a lot of people kayaking around Dubrovnik Castle. After my experience of getting out of one in Austin, I gave it a miss.

I also enjoyed walks in the area surrounding my hotel, where I stumbled upon little coves that were practically deserted, with many good spots for a swim.

As ever, getting the best views involves a cable car and there is one in Dubrovnik. Even though I knew there had been no accidents since it opened in 1969, I still couldn't look down on the way up, but then I'm a complete wuss. There's a snack bar and a nice restaurant at the top.

I had heard good things about Dubrovnik, but I was still pleasantly surprised at what a great place it was to go alone. Just don't blame me if you get stuck in a kayak.

Las Vegas

Yes, I know, I thought that too. For years, Las Vegas remained firmly off my list as only one word sprang to mind: 'tacky'. However, I had a hankering to see the Grand Canyon at least once in my lifetime, so off I went.

My daytimes in Vegas were spent by the pool, until it became unbearably hot, which was at approximately 9:37am each day. People will happily chat to you, and it was my first experience of being encouraged to drink alcohol *in* the pool. If you're coping well with the combination of jetlag, sun and booze, it's time to walk up and down the Strip, visiting various themed hotels, such as New York-New York Hotel & Casino, Paris Las Vegas and the Bellagio, if only for the famous fountains that you will have seen in every film set in Vegas.

As you get towards the end of the Strip, it becomes a bit more run-down and most visitors stick to the core area. American tourists are super friendly, and I counted that I spoke to ten different people one day, which I think is a record for me.

Of course, being in Vegas I had to try some slot machines. However, they only accepted notes, so it didn't feel *quite* like the movies. They provide you with free drinks while you play, so that helps you lose all sense of time and before you realise it their ploy has worked, and it is now 4am. I tried one machine at the MGM Grand while I was killing half an hour before going to see *The Lion King*. I won $1,200. The lights and bells went off and people came over to congratulate me. Two Irish lads couldn't believe I'd come to Vegas alone and was now sitting there with a minor jackpot win. It's certainly a clever way to make some new friends.

The evenings can be tricky when you holiday alone, but there is no shortage of entertainment to enjoy in Vegas. Many head there to see the big stars in residency. When I went, it was Bette Midler. While it's not quite like saying you've been to see Adele, she certainly put on a brilliant show. I had an enjoyable evening at *Phantom of the Opera, Vegas Spectacular*, followed by another at Penn & Teller's magic show, where I got to meet them both afterwards. I am aware that some people under 40 may now be busy looking up who they are. I also saw the actor and comedian Jon Lovitz doing stand-up, and one evening I joined a queue just to see what on earth was going on at the end of it. That's how I wound up meeting Marie Osmond. We had a nice little chat. She laughed when I said 'queue' rather than 'line', and signed the frightening doll from her collection which I had hastily purchased while in said queue/line. It just shows that anything can happen in Vegas.

Do try and experience the Grand Canyon if you can, though in the end it felt like a slightly soulless experience. If I did it again, I would try to do a few days hiking it with a group. Companies come to pick you up at your hotel and fly you over it in a helicopter, but you don't actually get to see that much. It's probably just one tiny corner. However, you do get to stop for some champagne and a photo with your pilot. You may even share the helicopter with Americans who ask if you have heard that a tunnel has been built between France and England. You try to look surprised.

I ended up going to Vegas a second time that year after a trip to San Francisco. It's definitely one of the easiest places to entertain yourself alone, and a good stopover when heading to the West Coast. You might even head home richer than when you arrived.

Bologna, Italy

The loveliest Italian man I have ever met once told me that I should go to Bologna, as it was a better place to visit than Florence. So, I did. Although I'm still not sure I agree, but I will forgive Antonio anything.

Bologna has a very different feel to Florence. It's bigger, and although I will usually just walk and walk, I had to relent and figure out how to use the buses to get around, even though porticos are provided as shade. It is certainly not as touristy as Florence. In fact, some of the tourist-related activities only run at weekends, so be careful not to get caught out.

Ravenna

Bologna

I found myself a nice place to stay, with a terrace and a hot tub (there are not a lot of hotel choices). If you are happy spending a lot of time on trains, it's a wonderful base for exploring some of the Emilia-Romagna region, as you can do the main sights of Bologna in a day.

My top things to see in Bologna are the Piazza Maggiore, which is somewhere to sit, eat your gelato and then hop on the tourist bus, which is worth it if you are short on time and want a good overview of the city and its history. It was while resting here that I noticed the town smelled heavily of pigeons, and then one promptly did its business down my shoulder. Thank goodness I always carry wet wipes. Ah, sweet holiday memories.

Take a look at the Two Towers of Bologna, which are both leaning. It's possible to climb to the top of one, which I heard is 498 steps. Even though, as you know, I love a good staircase, I had some concerns that the building looked like might be about to fall down, so I declined that particular activity.

Make sure you stop off at San Petronio, which is the 10th largest church in the world. You will need to cover your shoulders and legs to go inside. The Basilica of Santo Stefano is also very beautiful, just in case you haven't seen enough historical religious complexes by now. There's a very nice restaurant opposite.

It's easy to amble through the town centre, and nearly every street is gorgeous, although it was heavily bombed during the Second World War and you can see exactly where the bombs fell, due to newer buildings versus the old. Good shopping, great food and lots of elderly people smiling sweetly and saying hello in the street. There are plenty of museums too but, to be honest, I just couldn't be bothered. Mainly because it meant taking yet another bus, and I go to enough museums in London. Instead, I focused on doing some day trips by train from Bologna:

My first port of call was Parma, which is about an hour from Bologna. You can probably guess what it's famous for. Yes, parmesan and Parma ham. The town had a lovely feel to it, with lots of people on bikes and very few tourists even in July. I had been there for about 30 minutes before it started pouring. The weather in this area can be very changeable, even in the height of summer. Italians don't seem to carry umbrellas, so you will feel quite smug if you've brought yours with you. Book yourself on a wine tasting, and make sure you have room in your suitcase for plenty of cheese.

On my way back from Parma, I stopped off at Modena. Be prepared for a fairly long walk from the station to the centre, especially if it's humid and every step feels exhausting. Along the way were some of the most impressive buildings I have ever seen. It was super quiet: just me, some elderly people and many pigeons in the town square. I reached apprehensively for my wet wipes. Modena is not only the home of balsamic vinegar but also the late Luciano Pavarotti. There is a museum at his former home, but that required another bus or taxi and my energy was spent.

I debated long and hard about my final day trip. It was a toss-up between Ravenna and Ferrara. I chose Ravenna and I would later regret it when the train broke down in the tiny village of Lugo, which is in the middle of nowhere. I should have guessed this might happen, as I also always pick the wrong queue in supermarkets. Lugo was so small that the station did not possess a single employee to tell us what was happening. Looking online, we realised it was an electric fault and no trains were going in or out of the station. This was me and the other English- or French-speaking people I could find huddled on the platform, some who live one town away from me in London. It's a small world indeed.

After an hour waiting for a bus that never arrived, I ended up in a taxi with a couple from Belgium and an American student. When we finally made it to Ravenna, we were assured that the issues would be resolved by the time we needed to travel back to Bologna. The American student had to get to Rome that night, for her flight back to the US the next morning. Talk about tense moments. There was no choice but to head into Ravenna to see the mosaics in the meantime. You can buy a ticket in the Basilica di San Vitale ticket office or online, and they are all well worth a look.

Ravenna is a very pretty town, and the mosaics are beautiful. Some people travel across the world for this experience. I am obviously the only person who hasn't heard about them. We eventually got back to the station and, of course, there still weren't any trains. We had to fight our way through the crowds and the police, whom I assumed were there to protect the bus drivers from the baying mob. It transpired that their only duty was to check that the drivers had not been on the road for too many hours. We eventually made our way onto a bus, which proceeded to stop at every small town in the region before dumping us at a random train station about an hour from Bologna. What a day. We discussed whether we felt it had been worth it. Probably not.

With better public transport luck, this area is a super holiday by yourself. Although it's probably best not to attempt one of these trips on the day of your flight home.

Avignon and Provence, France

Avignon is not perhaps the most obvious of destinations, but was one of the most enjoyable. Since the pandemic and cuts to routes, it's harder to find a direct flight. The Eurostar is also an option, with a change in Paris to catch the high-speed rail service (the TGV) all the way there.

I stayed in a 16th-century building, which is apparently listed in the Register of Historical Monuments in France, although I'm not *totally* sure that the small swimming pool on the roof was an original feature. I went in June, and it was hot. That area regularly sees temperatures of around 40 degrees throughout the summer.

Avignon itself is a pretty town to wander around but the real appeal is that there are many tour companies that will come and take you out for the day.

I started by following in Vincent van Gogh's footsteps around the town of Arles, which is a UNESCO World Heritage Site and inspired many of his paintings. We stopped off at *Le Café van Gogh*, which you might recognise from his work *Café Terrace at Night*. That's fine, I'll wait while you look it up.

From there, we went to Les Baux-de-Provence, where we were taken to an old quarry for something called *Carrières de Lumières* (quarries of lights). No, at this point I was not massively impressed either. I mean, it's a quarry. We were taken inside and treated to an experience that has stayed with me ever since: a light and sound show featuring art works projected onto the walls, accompanied by very evocative music. In 2017 it included Bosch, Brueghel and Arcimboldo, among others. You can watch the video of that year, as well as others, on YouTube. At one point it appeared to be snowing on the quarry walls. I could have stayed for hours.

On the way home, we stopped at Saint-Rémy and the Saint-Paul Asylum. There are not many day trips that incorporate both a quarry *and* an asylum. Van Gogh was a self-admitted patient, and a collection of paintings reflect his time here.

Another trip took me to a little of the immense Parc Naturel Régional du Luberon, a truly idyllic landscape. The first stop in this area was Roussillon, described as 'the astonishing ochre village' due to the fact that every house is painted one of 17 approved shades. We then headed to Gordes, one of the most beautiful and well-known hilltop villages in France. Just soak it all in and it will stay in your memories forever.

I finished my trip with the main reason I was so keen to holiday in this area: to see the incredible lavender fields. We stopped off at Sénanque Abbey, which is surrounded by lavender, and then to random fields full of the stuff. It made for some wonderful photos. Be careful, as the lavender can only be seen from June until the beginning of August, and even that can depend on the weather. I met people who had been three times and never managed to see any, so I well and truly lucked out.

Sénanque Abbey

Gordes

Oh, how I loved this area. Avignon is a great base, and you will also meet lots of people on the excursions if you fancy some company. It's worth going for the lavender alone, and the countryside will make you want to start saving to spend more than *A Year in Provence*.

Like me, you may have dreamt about seeing whales in the wild. Did that dream also involve bobbing up and down for eight hours in what could generously be referred to as a tin can, with a guide regularly shouting things like 'Look, a great white shark!' or 'We saw the largest number of humpback whales we have *ever* seen yesterday'? They will feed you ginger to stop the sea sickness, and you'll jump every time a massive container ship appears out of the fog. But then, two magnificent humpback whales surface right next to the boat, and although their sheer size makes this a slightly terrifying experience, you will always remember it.

I tied in a San Francisco trip with going to Las Vegas, and spent four days there. There's quite a lot to keep you entertained. I started with Alcatraz Island, and took a boat over. I wasn't prepared for how cold and eerie it would feel, especially after the warmth of the city. It is also known as *The Rock*, and former inmates include the one and only Al Capone. You can have a little look at his cell.

When you've had enough of cold prisons, head to Yosemite National Park. It's a slightly tricky one without a car. There are companies that will take you for the day and leave you to wander round a small section, hoping you won't meet any bears. I would recommend staying there for at least a few days and using the park's public transportation to get around. If you're only there briefly, you will at least get to see El Capitan, the famous vertical rock formation that is instantly recognisable.

San Francisco

A fun activity is hiring a bike and cycling along the Golden Gate Bridge, which is over two miles long. Pick a clear day if you can. I did this alone, but a group might be more fun. You can pause to watch the huge container ships emerge from the mist. If you cycle all the way across, you'll end up in Sausalito for more views.

No trip to San Francisco is complete without a tour of Napa Valley. I will never forget that trip because of our guide, an extremely chirpy former actor from LA. Napa is surprisingly small at just a mile long. We stopped at several vineyards. Unsurprisingly, as the tastings went on, the jollier we all became.

As when visiting most American cities, you need to be careful about where you wander, and I don't believe the situation in San Francisco has improved since my trip.

I found myself in quite a dodgy area at one point, when I got lost on my way to the whale-watching trip but, luckily, I looked nothing like a tourist in my brand-new San Fran hoodie. Stick to the main tourist areas, and remember your sea sickness tablets.

Mykonos, Greece

I went to Mykonos for some late-May sun in 2016. I was surprised at how quiet it was. It appeared that the season hadn't started yet. As usual, my main reason for choosing this destination was that one of my favourite films, *Shirley Valentine*, was filmed there. This was the movie that made me want to travel. So, I felt I owed it to Mykonos, and to Shirley, to go. What do you mean, she's not a real person?

The island is incredibly beautiful, although run-down in areas due to lack of public funding. My hotel was right by the beach. I didn't realise so many people intended to sunbathe completely nude until I almost stood on them. It was a gorgeous little cove near the old fishing village of Panormos, with clear blue water and the sound of small fishing boats chugging gently through the sea.

I spent some time in Mykonos Town, spotting all the places my heroine Shirley had been to. This meant that I was possibly a little too excited about seeing a fish market. Make sure you stop off at the very famous windmills. There are 16 on the island, and they were designed to grind grain. These days, they are mainly used for getting a new profile picture, so good luck getting a shot of them with all the selfie sticks being waved around.

Mykonos

Mykonos

Beware of bumping into one of the town's famous pelicans as you wander through the streets. I had a 'back against the wall trying to get past without shrieking' moment attempting to get around one the size of a small elephant.

One note of caution regarding Mykonos airport, which is not equipped to deal with the number of tourists it receives during the summer (unless it has had a major upgrade by now). Leave plenty of time to get through. You'll also have to step over the stray cats lying all over the terminal floor.

Mykonos was hot, relaxing and the people were nice (if often starkers), but I did feel a bit isolated on my side of the island. The buses to the centre started up for the season during my stay, thank goodness. I would recommend being closer to the action if you can. I went to have a break from work and read books on the beach, but Mykonos Town is definitely more geared towards a vibrant nightlife. As well as the pelican community.

Toronto, Canada

I decided to visit Toronto over an August bank holiday weekend. The flight feels relatively short, and the lovely Air Canada crew must surely all have been part-time models.

The city of Toronto has a very new feel to it, with lots of shiny skyscrapers. There is excellent shopping but after the first day I realised that, as a Londoner, I didn't want to spend my holiday in another city and so the area I spent the most time in was Toronto Island Park.

The people who told me how packed the islands would be at the weekend have obviously never been to Brighton beach on that one hot day in May along with the rest of the country. I had a small beach to myself where I sat and watched Canada Geese (they would prefer that you don't refer to them as *Canadian.* I checked) and reflected on life. I recorded the quiet on my phone to listen to during rail strikes. I also hired a bike and rode around the island, accidentally catching a fleeting glimpse of the nudist beach as I passed.

Toronto

I decided to take in a baseball game. I arrived on time, ready to settle in, only to find that I was the only person there. It seems you come and go whenever you feel like it. The New York Yankees were playing the Toronto Blue Jays. People were walking around sporting T-shirts emblazoned with 'I love BJs'. Hmmm. I tried to get into the spirit and got myself a (vegetarian) hot dog and booed at A-Rod along with everyone else. There was no commentary though, so anything could have been happening down there. After an hour or so I made my excuses and left. The man who let me out informed me several times that I wouldn't be allowed back in. Honestly, that's *fine*.

No trip to Toronto is complete without a day trip to Niagara Falls. The Canadian side of the Falls is *so* much better than the US side, according to Canadians. Your life is not complete until you have been on the *Maid of the Mist* boat in a thunderstorm. My hair coped poorly with this experience. They provide a blue waterproof poncho, which serves as a nice souvenir. Just don't expect much else around the Falls, other than perhaps a coffee. We stopped off in a small town to sample wine and maple syrup on the way back. That was just fine and dandy with me.

Toronto is a great introduction to Canada but it's probably best to go during the summer, as their winters are harsh. Make sure you have some space in your luggage for all the syrup and the unintentionally pornographic T-shirts.

New York, USA

I first went to New York at 19, but only for a night on my way to Detroit. It was just after the release of the first *Austin Powers* movie and to be British in America at that time meant you were instantly the most popular person in the room.

It felt like I was on the set of a movie. Look at all those yellow cabs! I lay in my hostel listening to the dulcet sounds of shots being fired and I wasn't that keen on returning. However, I pulled myself together and, at the age of 27, found myself newly single and needing to get away. It's fair to say I was a little intimidated by this big city, and didn't venture that far off the main grid. I walked everywhere, as I couldn't figure out how the subway worked. When I went back for the third time at 35, I was a seasoned Londoner. By the end of my trip, I *owned* that subway.

There are, of course, endless things to see and do in New York, so whip out your guidebook and get on it. You can't miss Central Park, which I originally thought I could walk all the way around. No, I couldn't. It has a splendid ice rink at Christmas. I can't skate but watching people fall over is much more enjoyable. Take a walk across the Brooklyn Bridge and have lunch at Katz's Delicatessen, the deli that features in *When Harry Met Sally*. Spend your evenings at various Broadway show,s and sunny days at Coney Island, where you can ride the famous Wonder Wheel. I had '*One* ticket? Just *one?*' yelled at me, so I guess that means I was the first person to ever ride it alone since it opened in 1920.

Coney Island

New York

The Statue of Liberty on Ellis Island is a must-see, and do stop off at the museum there. Reading the stories of those who, despite the challenges, came to America to find a new life, will leave a big impression. Of course, the National 9/11 Memorial & Museum is a very popular site. It's up to you whether your heart can take it, but it felt important to me to pay my respects.

I would also recommend the New York Public Library, the Metropolitan Museum of Art, the Empire State Building and Top of the Rock for the views, Grand Central Terminal for people-watching, and the lesser-known New York City Fire Museum. It has an amazing collection of firefighting history and memorabilia, and is a lot quieter than the main museums.

If this still isn't enough, you can follow my lead and

track down the façade of the *Friends* building in Greenwich Village. Highlight of my entire life, never mind the trip.

I do love a bit of tennis, so I planned my last visit around the US Open. I've been to Wimbledon twice alone, so this was par for the course for me. It's actually easier to fly to New York to see the champions than it is to get into Wimbledon, which is just down the road from where I live. You can buy tickets online, or on the day if you queue. It's perhaps not quite as *refined* as Wimbledon. Think people eating hotdogs and resting their bare feet on the seat in front, rather than strawberries and formal jackets. To be honest, I just wanted to say I had been to the delightfully named Flushing Meadows.

New York will always be special to me, as the first place I realised I could go on holiday alone and have a fantastic time. This is just a taster of what this city has to offer. Get your walking shoes on, hope for an excellent exchange rate, and enjoy.

Majorca and Menorca, Spain

I have combined Majorca and Menorca, partly because they are close to each other geographically (I know this, but not where the Lake District is. Right), and also because they weren't my most successful holidays, through no fault of their own. It can happen, and that's OK. Nothing in life is perfect, and there will always be other holidays.

I went to Majorca in late September and stayed in the pretty little town of Pollensa. It's great for a few days, though quite quiet, especially out of season. I'm not convinced you should choose that area of Majorca for your very first trip away by yourself. When I go back, it will be to Palma, where there is more going on, and no having to take an hour-long bus ride at 5am to get back to the airport.

It started off well and I was enjoying reading my book on a sunbed, before taking a short boat trip to the beach at Formentor. It was on this boat that I began to feel a bit unwell. By the next day, I was in agony. I couldn't lie down without violent pain in my lungs. This meant that I could only sleep sitting up, which was a tad difficult.

I perched gingerly on a sunbed, putting my symptoms into the NHS Direct website, which told me to call an ambulance. It was Sunday and all the pharmacies were shut until Tuesday. Of course, I only had one painkiller with me, and rummaging around the bottom of my makeup bag proved fruitless. I had to wait until I got to the airport on Tuesday morning to buy some ibuprofen, and I managed the flight back to Gatwick in a tired stupor. It turned out I had developed pleurisy, which sounds like something from the Victorian era, but is in fact an infection of the outer lining of the lungs. I don't expect you ever thought you would learn so much from reading this book.

So yes, intense pain is my memory of Majorca, but it's the perfect place to go if you want a short-ish flight and sunshine. Before I became ill, I had been enjoying having my dinner at a lovely restaurant by the sea. The waiters didn't seem overly concerned that I was by myself, and I wasn't greeted with 'You are alone? Alone?' as I often am. Not all trips are perfect, and at least I still came back with a tan. However, I now always carry plenty of painkillers when travelling.

Now, on to Menorca. I wasn't ill on the trip, but the weather just didn't cooperate. I went at the beginning of May, and it was freezing. Grey, a bit wet. I spent the entire five days obsessing over how much nicer the weather was in Majorca, and why I hadn't gone there instead. There were four wool blankets in the cupboard of my apartment, and I slept under all of them.

The local town was pretty much shut up that early in the season, and I got through my books in record time. No Wi-Fi and no TV. No, this wasn't 1895. The coast looked beautiful, though, and seemed to be very popular with walkers. It felt a little lonely and bleak to me.

My tip for Menorca would be go later in the summer. It's probably a very good holiday, particularly if you own lots of proper walking gear (I do not).

The sun shone the day I left. Typical.

Majorca

Washington DC, USA

The first thing I noticed about DC is how compact it is. I had allowed myself three days there before heading to North Carolina to spend time with friends. I say 'friends' – I met a guy at a conference in the US who said that if I wanted to experience real southern hospitality, I should come and stay with him and his family. I'm not sure he realised I would be on the next plane over.

I started by paying a visit to The White House, which is smaller than I'd imagined. The museums in DC are among the best in the world, and also free. Not much in the US is, so make the most of it. I managed the Smithsonian and the National Air & Space Museum before walking to the US Capitol and the Lincoln Memorial.

The White House

Georgetown is a nice place to have lunch, with its cobblestone streets and university students milling about. I took the subway to the Pentagon and sat quietly at the 9/11 Memorial for a while. I stayed near the rather moving Arlington Cemetery. You can hop on a little bus, which takes you to the key 'sights' (it feels wrong saying that about a cemetery), including John F. Kennedy's grave. I'm pretty sure Elvis was on my bus. He really, *really* looked like him.

Georgetown

You can see most of Washington DC in one day, and the highlights just a few hours, but it's nice to allow a little extra time to take in some of the museums too. It's also very easy to get around, and so I walked most of it. You may want to consider combining a trip to DC with other US destinations. And don't forget to say hi to Elvis.

Costa del Sol, Spain

I sometimes struggle with inspiration for a sun holiday. Much as I love Nice, I occasionally try to broaden my horizons. In May, I am usually looking for somewhere hot and within two hours' flight time.

I had been contemplating the Costa del Sol for a while, and was hoping to go to Nerja or Grenada, as I've always wanted to see the Alhambra. However, it seemed a bit of a slog when I just wanted a relaxing break. I decided to stay near Puerto Banús, which isn't far from Marbella. So off I went in May 2017, hoping for some early summer sun.

On arrival, it was grey, wet, and the only time I've seen such big waves was in *The Perfect Storm*. I wanted to cry. As did the two blokes I shared a taxi with ('I've not come all the way from Sheffield for this'). I spent the next few days obsessively checking the weather forecast. Eventually the sun did come out.

Puerto Banús

I had two main activities other than meteorological preoccupation. The first was walking. There is a wonderful coastal path that takes you to Puerto Banús one way and to Marbella the other. It takes about an hour to walk to Marbella, which I did on one occasion.

Once there, I headed straight for the Old Town. The endless whitewashed buildings with balconies covered in flowers were what my soul needed. I bought an ice cream in the shape of a flower and then headed back along the coastal path. The rest of the town seemed to be endless high-rises and that just isn't my cup of tea.

On the other side of my hotel was Puerto Banús, which is fairly exclusive. I definitely couldn't afford to dine out there. I had a quick stroll past the very expensive shops before I returned to my weather-watching. You may catch a glimpse of some of the cast of *TOWIE* there, as it is apparently their destination of choice when not in Dubai.

My second activity was going to the ALDI opposite my hotel. That's about as good as it got. I would go back and explore more of that area but next time suck it up and travel further along the coast. Whether this is your type of trip really depends on what you're looking for from a holiday. If it's spotting the stars of a British reality show, then go for it.

Orlando, USA

Orlando had been on my to-do list for a couple of years. More in a sense of 'I might as well cross it off' than any real desire to actually go there. I wondered if it might seem a bit strange for an adult to visit the parks alone, but my small relatives

Universal Studios

Magic Kingdom

were too tiny to go and, for some reason, no one wanted to lend me their kid. I also thought about what this trip would be like for someone who hates rollercoasters, or any ride with more velocity than the teacups.

I really didn't know what to expect. I had some time off between jobs in January, and thought it might be sunny with lots to do. I had been slightly frightened by the sight of so many small children waiting to board the Orlando flight on previous Gatwick trips. However, in the end, January was the best possible time to go child-wise as they were all in school. I even got a row of seats on the plane to myself. Both ways.

Until I started looking into Orlando, I didn't understand how the parks were laid out. I didn't realise that the Wizarding World of Harry Potter was part of Universal Studios. I had never even heard of Disney's Animal Kingdom. And I was definitely in no way prepared for the wait times, which I continued to check obsessively on an app for several months following my trip.

Off I went, leaving behind the grey winter. I will now impart everything I learnt.

Hotels and travel

There are *many* hotels to choose from but think about basing yourself near the park(s) where you are likely to spend the most time. I stayed near Universal, but only had one day there, costing me quite a lot in Uber rides.

Most hotels offer free shuttles to the parks and, if you are not planning on hiring a car, this is certainly worthwhile. You pay it back in local taxes, so that's nice.

Unless you plan on having every meal at your accommodation, check whether there are any stores or restaurants nearby before you book. I discovered that it is very hard to find any kind of vegetable, or vegetarian food, in Orlando – other than peppers on pizza. That bruised apple at the bottom of your handbag suddenly looks quite enticing.

Universal Studios Florida

There are three parks: Universal Studios, Islands of Adventure and Volcano Bay (which I didn't do).

Now, if you want the full Harry Potter experience, you will need to purchase a two-park pass. They have cannily put Hogsmeade in one park and Diagon Alley in another, with the Hogwarts Express running between the two (you can go back and forth). In January 2018, this pass cost around £130 for *one day*. Yes, you will be spending quite a lot of money while you're there.

I'm a bit of a Potterhead and so this was the absolute highlight of my trip. I tried a ride called *Escape from Gringotts*, even though I was petrified. I learnt soon afterwards that there are signs at the entrance to each ride telling you what to expect. I hadn't been paying attention so then, of course, totally enjoyed being plunged vertically through a black hole on a roller coaster. I still feel bad for that man and his kids who had to listen to me screaming next to them. The attention to detail is amazing. The goblins in Gringotts, the very realistic King's Cross station, and a conversation with the one and only Stan Shunpike. If only it had been raining, it would have felt just like home.

As you arrive at Universal, there is the City Walk, which has restaurants, shops, cinemas, etc., and is free. Make the most of it as it's pretty much the only place that is.

I enjoyed Universal most. It had the best rides, although I was too much of a wuss to try many. If you ask a park employee, they will recommend what they call the 'tame' rides. I tried *King Kong: Skull Island* on their advice, and only shut my eyes once. Also, the wait times were not quite as long as at Disney.

If you go on a water ride, you will get wet. From what I observed, not just a bit wet but absolutely drenched. There are even 'people dryers', which are massive hair dryers that you stand in as they blast you. You have been warned.

Walt Disney World Resort

There are four parks at Disney World: Magic Kingdom, Epcot, Animal Kingdom and Hollywood Studios, which I didn't go to on the advice of others.

Magic Kingdom. I went to the holy grail of all things Disney on a sunny Tuesday morning and took the ferry to the entrance, rather than the monorail. You have the choice: the ferry is slower but more fun. Wrap up warm if it's 8:30am in January though, as even Florida can be a little chilly out on the water.

I got there early but it was already packed. Think Oxford Street on Boxing Day vibes.

I know people who love Disney so much they go every year. Yes, the Cinderella Castle is cool, and if you feel like waiting in line for ages there are some good rides, although several were closed that day. However, particularly after Universal, it all felt a bit tired and dated, and not particularly magical. Although I'm not sure single, 39-year-old women are their target audience.

I take my hat off to folks who take their kids to the Magic Kingdom. There must be some kind of bravery award in existence for that. After three hours, an hour of which was spent with small children spilling juice on the back of my legs while I waited for the *Peter Pan* ride, I was done.

Epcot. This stands for Experimental Prototype Community of Tomorrow (obviously). I was pleasantly surprised by Epcot. I did my favourite ride there – *Soarin'*. Yay, heights and 3D! Finally, something I can get on board with. I also enjoyed walking round the 11 international pavilions, which consist of a stereotypical building or two from the likes of London (a fish and chip shop), Paris, Venice and so on. Mary Poppins was hanging about in London, so all dreams *do* come true. This was confirmed when I managed to find a vegetarian wrap in the food hall.

Animal Kingdom. Everyone, from the concierge to my Uber Driver Joel from Haiti, told me about the *Avatar: Flight of Passage* ride, which people apparently queue up to eight hours for. On the day I went, the wait time was three hours. Talk about lucky! I've never seen *Avatar*, so I wasn't that fussed, but then you see all these people waiting and wonder 'What's that all about, then?'

I decided to pose that very question to a Disney employee and after a bit of chit-chat, she realised I was alone and handed me two FastPasses to use on both the Avatar rides (the other is the *Na'vi* boat ride). *Boom*! I'll admit I had been hoping this would be the outcome of the conversation. Afterwards, I wondered if I should have sold the passes for a tidy sum. Ah well. The boat ride wasn't really worth it, but *Flight of Passage* was. My eyes were shut for some of the fastest bits, but I have since watched it on YouTube to see what I missed.

Alligators

No, this isn't another theme park (although I almost wish it was). You can't go to Florida without seeing some gators. My concierge booked me onto a trip to *Wild Florida* where I was able to achieve my dream of riding in an air boat and seeing gators in their natural habitat. The air boat was faster than any ride at Universal, with the spicy addition of animals that could kill you circling the craft.

Alligators are apparently pretty stupid, and if one spots you, the best thing to do is go towards it as they can't see you head-on. Just like in *Jurassic Park*. Luckily, I didn't have to test this theory. Wild Florida also has a nice little animal park where you can observe rescue gators, who had previously been living in bath tubs. Personally, I can think of better pets.

This trip was also memorable for the fact that, as we were leaving, our driver hit another van and we had to spend two hours standing about talking about British politics while waiting for the local sheriff.

General tips

If you are a bit scared about the rides, I would suggest watching ones you are not sure about on YouTube first. I wish I had done that. Though I might not have got on the ones I did manage if I had.

If you are there for more than a week, or you don't fancy the main parks, investigate what else that area of Florida has to offer. There are plenty of other things to do and Uber will help you get around without a car. Speak to your concierge, as some companies will do a local pick-up. I haven't mentioned SeaWorld and that's because I have seen the film *Blackfish*.

Make use of the Disney MagicMobile Service in the My Disney Experience app. You can view the layouts of the parks and link your tickets to it. You can also get yourself ready for the wait times and, now that they have done away with the FastPass system, look into new ways of giving the Walt Disney Company even more of your money to avoid the queues.

I wasn't prepared for how into Disney some adults are. The customised T-shirts on 40-something men are a sight to behold. This is serious business in America.

I probably wouldn't go back to Orlando but I'm glad I did it once in my life. Although, if they expand their Harry Potter offering, I may have to rethink that.

Venice, Italy

It was January, and I needed to use up some holiday, so I thought I would give Venice a try. I was greeted by cold weather but clear blue skies, and I felt like George and Amal as I arrived by water taxi. I'm pretty sure theirs was better than mine. I'm certain their hotel room was better than mine, which was the size of a coffin.

Venice is a great place for a city break. There is just so much to see and explore. I quite enjoyed playing 'Spot the gondola engagement moment', with an average of around five a day.

Venice

You need to be comfortable with walking quite a bit, and the centre seems like a maze. I mainly stuck to the key tourist spots. This was one break where I didn't even feel ashamed to look like a visitor. Even with my map and phone, I kept ending up in random streets that didn't seem to lead anywhere. Two years later I went back with someone who used to live in Venice. What a difference it makes having a guide with you who really knows the place. No more tourist-only restaurants for me! Although the water smelt a little worse in May than it had in January.

Anyway, back to my solo trip. My favourite spots were the Rialto Bridge at night, St Mark's Campanile, the Peggy Guggenheim Collection, St Mark's Square and the Basilica di San Marco, which is totally touristy but I loved it anyway.

Get to know the vaporetto boat routes. They are not as difficult to navigate as they might seem. Take one over to the island of Murano, which is famous for its glass and also beautiful to walk around, even if you don't make it to the glass factory. If you do, take your credit card. I didn't get to the island of Burano, but it looks very pretty from the pictures.

Probably best to get to Venice sooner rather than later, just in case it ends up under water in the future.

Santorini, Greece

I had put off visiting Santorini, as it seemed to be a honeymooner's paradise, and who wants to be confronted by other people's happiness as you mooch about by yourself eating endless ice creams?

Me, that's who. If I can do it in Venice, I can do it in Santorini.

Yes, there is quite a lot of that. It's also not the *cheapest* holiday. The flights are extortionate. I think I have flown to New York for less. Off I went at the end of May to find blue skies and black sand beaches. I stayed near Perissa, in the south of the island. I had no hope of affording a hotel in Oia or Fira, the two main tourist hubs that you see in all the photos, their pristine whitewashed buildings overlooking the turquoise sea.

Santorini

Santorini

You can get local buses very easily around Santorini, and I quickly learnt to pay *after* sitting down. I went to Oia first, which is definitely the most beautiful spot. Everyone wants their photo taken here. It can be a little difficult getting the perfect shot while large groups of cruise ship passengers push past as though you're invisible. If you can ignore the crowds, it is a really special place that looks exactly like it does in the pictures.

Fira is the capital of the island and also gorgeous. Spend a day wandering the streets, take in the excellent Museum of Prehistoric Thira, and have lunch at one of their superb restaurants. One thing that did deduct quite a few brownie points from me was the poor donkeys being made to carry tourists up a hill. I'm not terribly fit but didn't find it that challenging. There is absolutely no need to clamber onto a donkey.

There seemed to be a few other places to visit if you were keen to sit on more hot buses, such as Akrotiri, and some beautiful vineyards. Crete is also only four hours away by ferry, but Santorini can be windy, and the sea didn't look that inviting.

I find relaxing properly quite difficult, but I had no choice in Santorini. It's actively encouraged, and so three whole days were spent around the pool and on the beach, and one whole book was read.

Go, relax, and remember that 42% of marriages end in divorce.

Frasier and *Sleepless in Seattle*. I studied hard before this holiday.

One easy nine-and-a-half-hour flight later, there I was. It was simple to get the train from the airport into town too, if you don't mind dragging your luggage up a few steep hills. Just don't let go of your case.

As expected, Seattle was a bit grey, even though it was June. They get rather a lot of rain there. My trusty umbrella saw quite a lot of action. The main attraction seemed to be the first ever *Starbucks*, with people queuing up to take photos. I'm not sure how interested others will be in those photos, but who am I to judge. Maybe as I rarely drink coffee, I just didn't get it.

I visited the famous Pike Place market and then went to the top of the iconic Space Needle, also known as Seattle's Eiffel Tower. You'll recognise it from the Seattle skyline at the beginning of *Frasier*. It's not quite as terrifying as some of the other buildings I have challenged myself to stand at the top of.

I booked a trip to go orca watching and I'll never forget it. The boat took us to the coast of Canada, and I met some lovely Americans as we sipped hot drinks down below. We then stood on the top deck, holding our collective breath to see where a momma whale and her baby would resurface while, of course, maintaining a very respectable distance from them. So far, that they could have simply been quite large fish. I also enjoyed the screams from the people in the

Seattle

tiny boats minding their own business and having a nice day out, when the orcas surfaced right next to them. 'You're going to need a bigger boat.'

A lot of people rave about Seattle and perhaps the weather diminished my experience a little. I had probably been watching too much *Twilight* and had begun to romanticise damp weather. That can happen, I guess.

From what I could see from the boat on my whale-watching trip, I suspect that the areas surrounding the city are pretty incredible, so get out there if you can. If you've been watching *Free Willy* lately, it's the place for you.

The Algarve, Portugal

Back in the carefree days of our early thirties, a university friend and I rocked up in the Algarve for a few days and did nothing but lounge about in the sun and chat, with the occasional trip to a shop or restaurant. In May 2023, I went back by myself to explore a little further.

My pal and I had based ourselves in Vilamoura, so this time I decided to try a new spot. I settled on the pretty traditional fishing town of Olhão, which is only 20 minutes from Faro airport. I hopped on a flight from Heathrow with 40 Portuguese teenagers, returning from a school trip. British Airways were kind enough to seat me in the middle of this group. One of the stewards looked at me and said: 'This is going to be a long flight. And *I* used to be a teacher.'

Luckily, most of them dozed off quite quickly and we arrived without fuss. I just *love* stepping from the airport terminal into warmth, and shrugging off the layers from another cold, wet winter. The weather was glorious for the whole week, and I spent a lot of time on my terrace, reading and catching glimpses of the Coronation on my phone.

However, I also wanted to see a little more of this area, and my driver had advised a trip to a town called Tavira. I went to explore Olhão's train station, and quickly realised there were no departure boards. My phone informed me of the time of the next train, but it didn't seem terribly accurate. When trains do decide to turn up, you don't know which platform they will arrive at. So, if you're on the wrong one, you run across the tracks behind it. I resisted shouting something about Health & Safety to the locals, for whom this was completely normal.

I had a look around Tavira, which is indeed very pretty, and sat on the bridge overlooking the water, listening to a busker play a mournful violin. I messaged my family to say I felt I was about to go down on *Titanic*. I then visited the majestic Santa Maria do Castelo Church, and sat on a pew to watch some of the ongoing restoration work. You step back in time as you go through the door, and I almost had the place to myself. If I had been in a film, another lone traveller would have wandered in, and the greatest love story of our time would have begun. Or perhaps I just have an overactive imagination.

I also caught a train to Faro, where I met another solo female traveller, and we walked into town together. I didn't feel there was a huge amount to see there, but I did enjoy the area around the Cathedral of Faro. However, my new friend and I were both back on the train within two hours.

Olhão

Another day trip was to Armona island. There are boats from Olhão to three islands: Armona, Culatra and Farol, known as 'the sandbank islands'. The timetables in early May were still either on spring or winter, despite it being 35 degrees, and so I only made it to Armona. I had read an article in *The Guardian* by a journalist who spent lockdown on Armona. It is certainly very charming. There are no cars, only long stretches of sand and pretty holiday homes. I sat on the beach for a while and watched a dog having the time of its life in the water, before I caught the return ferry.

You can travel all along that coast without a car, but I was content to stay in Olhão for the rest of my time. I fell in love with this little spot. There weren't too many tourists, it felt safe, and it was incredibly easy to go to restaurants along its marina by myself. There were a lot of apartments being built, and I just hope it doesn't become the new Albufeira.

I couldn't recommend the Algarve more for a holiday alone, and I'm hoping to go back later this year. I keep telling myself that, one day, I too will live somewhere where orange trees line the streets.

Additional ideas for solo holidays

When you're trying to tick off holiday destinations by only using your annual leave allowance, it takes some time to get around everywhere you want to go.

If you need further ideas, I still intend to check off Amsterdam, Lisbon, Sedona, Fuerteventura, Split, Corsica, Montréal, Vancouver, the Alhambra, Copenhagen, Madeira and every Greek island and US state that I haven't yet visited (I have only done 13 so this will take some effort).

There are also quite a few places I have holidayed with other people that I would return to alone, including Edinburgh, Paris, Geneva, Zurich, Rhodes and Tenerife.

If you happen to have more than a week or two free, you might want to holiday further afield. I can certainly recommend New Zealand as a destination, if you can bear the long flights. It's so much more than sheep.

I decided to move there when I was 24. The things you do when you're young. I ended up in Christchurch on the South Island. There weren't many people my age in

Christchurch, as most seemed to be doing their own 'Big OE' (Overseas Experience) in Europe. This meant that at weekends and on holidays, I mainly hung out alone (get used to it, love, this won't be the last time). My little blue Suzuki Vitara, imaginatively named Suzi, and I had many adventures together until an elderly couple drove into the back of her.

As I was working, I didn't have as much time for sightseeing as I had hoped, but I still enjoyed several minibreaks during my year there and I recommend the following places.

Milford Sound. It took about nine hours on a bus from Christchurch to get there. It was worth it to take a trip on the water through this fjord, which was once described by Rudyard Kipling as the 'eighth wonder of the world'.

Wellington. The capital city of New Zealand, which everyone thinks is Auckland. Sadly, it was wet and grey during my trip. Make sure you go to the national museum of New Zealand, Te Papa Tongarewa. Take a ride on the cable car, explore the beaches if you get good weather, and enjoy the fact that it's the culinary capital of New Zealand.

Queenstown. I spent Easter here, and it was one of the coldest places I have ever visited. If you don't mind how glacial it is, and enjoy water sports, this is the place for you. I don't, so I spent an inordinate amount of time at the cinema watching *Johnny English*.

Kaikoura. You can go whale-watching here, unless the weather is too bad in full summer, and it gets called off. Nearly 20 years later and I'm still annoyed about that. If this happens, spend your time at the Kaikoura Wine Company instead. Not only will the wine help you forget your frustration, but you might just see a whale in the distance from their gardens.

Hanmer Springs Thermal Pools and Spa. This is an amazing spot with incredible views for a day out by yourself, though you might overheat a little in the summer.

Sumner. A really lovely beach just outside Christchurch, where you could easily spend a long weekend. It is also where I got sunburnt on Christmas Day that year.

New Zealand is a great destination for a holiday alone, provided you have at least three weeks to enjoy it. Head there during their summer, which is our winter. A car is recommended and it's a very easy place to get around. As soon as you start driving, you see the most incredible scenery and understand why *Lord of the Rings* was filmed there. Its reputation as a place of beauty is well-deserved.

When you live in New Zealand, where else are you going to go on holiday, but Australia. Before I moved back to Europe, I decided to take a brief holiday alone to Oz. My first stop was Sydney. It was strange to be in a big city again, after the relative ruralness of New Zealand. I did all the main sights, including the Sydney Opera House, Bondi

Beach, Sydney Harbour, the beach-side suburb of Manly, and various galleries and museums.

From Sydney, I flew to Cairns to see the Great Barrier Reef. Here, I encountered the biggest spider I have ever seen, hanging over the entrance to the pool at the hotel. I talked it into remaining still as I tried to duck under it. It was actually fairly obedient. I spent the rest of the trip checking my bed, clothes, shoes, curtains, shower, *everything* for spiders – or worse.

Taking a break from hiding under the covers, I jumped on a boat with 50 American tourists to snorkel on the Reef. What they don't tell you is that the likelihood of being sick on that boat is around 99%. Suddenly all that could be heard was the sound of retching. Somehow, I managed not to vomit, and was informed that the best thing to do to get over the nausea was to jump in the water and start snorkelling. This turned out to be factually accurate.

It was June, the water was low, and the coral looked brown and not very healthy. In my wiser, post-*Blue Planet* days, I now know this isn't a good sign. So perhaps give that one a miss and contribute towards its preservation instead.

Random tips that you may or may not appreciate

SIX

Here are some final titbits I have learnt over the years, which might make your holiday alone that little bit more successful.

Obviously, it's up to you how you spend your money, but I would recommend choosing to spend your hard-earned cash on experiences rather than material things when you're away. That T-shirt from New York might not fit in five years' time, but you'll always remember the view from the top of the Empire State Building.

It's hard to find an open supermarket in European countries on Sunday afternoons, particularly in rural areas. If you arrive on that day, make sure you pick up some food at the airport, especially if you're staying somewhere that doesn't offer room service or have a restaurant. Also, check to see if there are any public holidays coming up, when once again everything is shut and all you have to eat is the warm egg sandwich you bought at *Boots* in Gatwick.

Always pack some wooden cutlery so you have the option of eating a yogurt in your hotel room in the morning, rather than pay 18 Euros to pick at a dry croissant in the restaurant.

Websites such as *Viator* are your friend for finding day trips from your location and helping get you out and about without having to worry about hiring a car. I always have a quick check before I book a destination, just to see what the options are.

Don't be afraid to get in touch with your accommodation to ask for a quiet room, or one with lots of sun, if that will make you happier. Equally, don't be afraid to speak up if something isn't right. There's nothing worse than spending the week in a room next to one taken up by members of a rowdy stag party.

Over time, you will learn to pack a capsule wardrobe. Bring some detergent to rinse items like swimwear in the sink. Some lodgings provide washing machines, and you then experience the unadulterated joy of coming home with a suitcase of clean clothes. If I can manage nine days in Miami with only hand luggage, anything is possible.

There are discounts available on pretty much everything, so don't forget to shop around, from hotel rooms to transfers and my favourite hop-on, hop-off buses.

If you have the spare cash, it's worth booking a seat on your flight ahead of time on long-haul. Since I spent 14 hours in the dreaded middle seat on a flight to Buenos Aires, surrounded by two burly men, I never forget to do this. I like an aisle seat on the way out, so I don't have to clamber over someone every time I need to stretch my legs to save my swollen ankles. On the return flight, I always book a window seat if it's a night flight, so you can snuggle up against it to sleep instead of dribbling on the shoulder of the stranger next to you.

If you're struggling to find your way to an attraction and are in doubt about where you're going, you can be pretty sure that if you just follow other people, you'll get to whatever you're trying to find. Or you'll just end up at someone's house. Hopefully they won't mind.

SEVEN
And now...over to you

I hope that I have provided you with enough inspiration and advice for a successful solo holiday and that you are now busy ordering a travel guide or two. If that's the case, I'm very proud of you. You have shed society's preconceptions and my job here is done.

Yes, I certainly know how lucky I am. I have had the opportunity to experience things I never thought I would. Travel has been my main hobby over the years, and I figure that, if it costs about a quarter of a million pounds to raise a child, I can spend my money on holidays instead.

If you don't feel quite ready yet, that's OK. Even though I have been on trips alone frequently, I still have to psych myself up, particularly for the more far-flung destinations. There are times when it feels that it would indeed be easier to stay home and watch Wimbledon. But then this book would have been quite boring.

It's definitely more of an effort to motivate yourself to go alone, as you have to be completely responsible for yourself the whole time you're away. However, I'm always glad I made myself do it. When I look back at each of these holidays, I reflect on how much these experiences have shaped me as a person. I don't think I would have become who I am today if I hadn't taken the chance and driven through Texas that time. You will get so much out of it, and the trips you take will provide memories that will last the rest of your life.

If an entire holiday by yourself doesn't appeal, incorporate something like a yoga retreat or a walking tour with a group. I understand that most people aren't as anti-social as me, and don't necessarily believe that 'Hell is other people'.

Don't wait for others in order to do the things you've always wanted to. Enjoy marching to the beat of your own drum. Go while you're still in good health and mobile, as getting older creeps up on us all, much as we like to think we will be forever young. As the author Jack Kornfield, in *Buddha's Little Instruction Book*, says, 'The trouble is, you think you have time'. Don't have regrets about not taking the chance.

If nothing else, you could learn some essential facts about random places that might one day help you win a pub quiz. You'll also end up with a really attractive collection of travel books on your living room shelf.

I am with you; you can do this. And if you see me on a sun lounger next to you, I don't even mind if you say hello.